MW00397657

FREE Test Taking Tips DVD Offer

To help us better serve you, we have developed a Test Taking Tips DVD that we would like to give you for FREE. **This DVD covers world-class test taking tips that you can use to be even more successful when you are taking your test.**

All that we ask is that you email us your feedback about your study guide. Please let us know what you thought about it – whether that is good, bad or indifferent.

To get your **FREE Test Taking Tips DVD**, email freedvd@studyguideteam.com with "FREE DVD" in the subject line and the following information in the body of the email:

    a. The title of your study guide.

    b. Your product rating on a scale of 1-5, with 5 being the highest rating.

    c. Your feedback about the study guide. What did you think of it?

    d. Your full name and shipping address to send your free DVD.

If you have any questions or concerns, please don't hesitate to contact us at freedvd@studyguideteam.com.

Thanks again!

FSA Grade 3 ELA Practice Book

3rd Grade FSA Test Prep Florida & Practice Questions for the Florida Standards Assessment [Includes Detailed Answer Explanations]

Test Prep Books

Copyright © 2019 Test Prep Books

All rights reserved.

Table of Contents

Quick Overview

As you draw closer to taking your exam, effective preparation becomes more and more important. Thankfully, you have this study guide to help you get ready. Use this guide to help keep your studying on track and refer to it often.

This study guide contains several key sections that will help you be successful on your exam. The guide contains tips for what you should do the night before and the day of the test. Also included are test-taking tips. Knowing the right information is not always enough. Many well-prepared test takers struggle with exams. These tips will help equip you to accurately read, assess, and answer test questions.

A large part of the guide is devoted to showing you what content to expect on the exam and to helping you better understand that content. In this guide are practice test questions so that you can see how well you have grasped the content. Then, answer explanations are provided so that you can understand why you missed certain questions.

Don't try to cram the night before you take your exam. This is not a wise strategy for a few reasons. First, your retention of the information will be low. Your time would be better used by reviewing information you already know rather than trying to learn a lot of new information. Second, you will likely become stressed as you try to gain a large amount of knowledge in a short amount of time. Third, you will be depriving yourself of sleep. So be sure to go to bed at a reasonable time the night before. Being well-rested helps you focus and remain calm.

Be sure to eat a substantial breakfast the morning of the exam. If you are taking the exam in the afternoon, be sure to have a good lunch as well. Being hungry is distracting and can make it difficult to focus. You have hopefully spent lots of time preparing for the exam. Don't let an empty stomach get in the way of success!

When travelling to the testing center, leave earlier than needed. That way, you have a buffer in case you experience any delays. This will help you remain calm and will keep you from missing your appointment time at the testing center.

Be sure to pace yourself during the exam. Don't try to rush through the exam. There is no need to risk performing poorly on the exam just so you can leave the testing center early. Allow yourself to use all of the allotted time if needed.

Remain positive while taking the exam even if you feel like you are performing poorly. Thinking about the content you should have mastered will not help you perform better on the exam.

Once the exam is complete, take some time to relax. Even if you feel that you need to take the exam again, you will be well served by some down time before you begin studying again. It's often easier to convince yourself to study if you know that it will come with a reward!

Test-Taking Strategies

1. Predicting the Answer

When you feel confident in your preparation for a multiple-choice test, try predicting the answer before reading the answer choices. This is especially useful on questions that test objective factual knowledge. By predicting the answer before reading the available choices, you eliminate the possibility that you will be distracted or led astray by an incorrect answer choice. You will feel more confident in your selection if you read the question, predict the answer, and then find your prediction among the answer choices. After using this strategy, be sure to still read all of the answer choices carefully and completely. If you feel unprepared, you should not attempt to predict the answers. This would be a waste of time and an opportunity for your mind to wander in the wrong direction.

2. Reading the Whole Question

Too often, test takers scan a multiple-choice question, recognize a few familiar words, and immediately jump to the answer choices. Test authors are aware of this common impatience, and they will sometimes prey upon it. For instance, a test author might subtly turn the question into a negative, or he or she might redirect the focus of the question right at the end. The only way to avoid falling into these traps is to read the entirety of the question carefully before reading the answer choices.

3. Looking for Wrong Answers

Long and complicated multiple-choice questions can be intimidating. One way to simplify a difficult multiple-choice question is to eliminate all of the answer choices that are clearly wrong. In most sets of answers, there will be at least one selection that can be dismissed right away. If the test is administered on paper, the test taker could draw a line through it to indicate that it may be ignored; otherwise, the test taker will have to perform this operation mentally or on scratch paper. In either case, once the obviously incorrect answers have been eliminated, the remaining choices may be considered. Sometimes identifying the clearly wrong answers will give the test taker some information about the correct answer. For instance, if one of the remaining answer choices is a direct opposite of one of the eliminated answer choices, it may well be the correct answer. The opposite of obviously wrong is obviously right! Of course, this is not always the case. Some answers are obviously incorrect simply because they are irrelevant to the question being asked. Still, identifying and eliminating some incorrect answer choices is a good way to simplify a multiple-choice question.

4. Don't Overanalyze

Anxious test takers often overanalyze questions. When you are nervous, your brain will often run wild, causing you to make associations and discover clues that don't actually exist. If you feel that this may be a problem for you, do whatever you can to slow down during the test. Try taking a deep breath or counting to ten. As you read and consider the question, restrict yourself to the particular words used by the author. Avoid thought tangents about what the author *really* meant, or what he or she was *trying* to say. The only things that matter on a multiple-choice test are the words that are actually in the question. You must avoid reading too much into a multiple-choice question, or supposing that the writer meant something other than what he or she wrote.

5. No Need for Panic

It is wise to learn as many strategies as possible before taking a multiple-choice test, but it is likely that you will come across a few questions for which you simply don't know the answer. In this situation, avoid panicking. Because most multiple-choice tests include dozens of questions, the relative value of a single wrong answer is small. As much as possible, you should compartmentalize each question on a multiple-choice test. In other words, you should not allow your feelings about one question to affect your success on the others. When you find a question that you either don't understand or don't know how to answer, just take a deep breath and do your best. Read the entire question slowly and carefully. Try rephrasing the question a couple of different ways. Then, read all of the answer choices carefully. After eliminating obviously wrong answers, make a selection and move on to the next question.

6. Confusing Answer Choices

When working on a difficult multiple-choice question, there may be a tendency to focus on the answer choices that are the easiest to understand. Many people, whether consciously or not, gravitate to the answer choices that require the least concentration, knowledge, and memory. This is a mistake. When you come across an answer choice that is confusing, you should give it extra attention. A question might be confusing because you do not know the subject matter to which it refers. If this is the case, don't eliminate the answer before you have affirmatively settled on another. When you come across an answer choice of this type, set it aside as you look at the remaining choices. If you can confidently assert that one of the other choices is correct, you can leave the confusing answer aside. Otherwise, you will need to take a moment to try to better understand the confusing answer choice. Rephrasing is one way to tease out the sense of a confusing answer choice.

7. Your First Instinct

Many people struggle with multiple-choice tests because they overthink the questions. If you have studied sufficiently for the test, you should be prepared to trust your first instinct once you have carefully and completely read the question and all of the answer choices. There is a great deal of research suggesting that the mind can come to the correct conclusion very quickly once it has obtained all of the relevant information. At times, it may seem to you as if your intuition is working faster even than your reasoning mind. This may in fact be true. The knowledge you obtain while studying may be retrieved from your subconscious before you have a chance to work out the associations that support it. Verify your instinct by working out the reasons that it should be trusted.

8. Key Words

Many test takers struggle with multiple-choice questions because they have poor reading comprehension skills. Quickly reading and understanding a multiple-choice question requires a mixture of skill and experience. To help with this, try jotting down a few key words and phrases on a piece of scrap paper. Doing this concentrates the process of reading and forces the mind to weigh the relative importance of the question's parts. In selecting words and phrases to write down, the test taker thinks about the question more deeply and carefully. This is especially true for multiple-choice questions that are preceded by a long prompt.

9. Subtle Negatives

One of the oldest tricks in the multiple-choice test writer's book is to subtly reverse the meaning of a question with a word like *not* or *except*. If you are not paying attention to each word in the question, you can easily be led astray by this trick. For instance, a common question format is, "Which of the following is...?" Obviously, if the question instead is, "Which of the following is not...?," then the answer will be quite different. Even worse, the test makers are aware of the potential for this mistake and will include one answer choice that would be correct if the question were not negated or reversed. A test taker who misses the reversal will find what he or she believes to be a correct answer and will be so confident that he or she will fail to reread the question and discover the original error. The only way to avoid this is to practice a wide variety of multiple-choice questions and to pay close attention to each and every word.

10. Reading Every Answer Choice

It may seem obvious, but you should always read every one of the answer choices! Too many test takers fall into the habit of scanning the question and assuming that they understand the question because they recognize a few key words. From there, they pick the first answer choice that answers the question they believe they have read. Test takers who read all of the answer choices might discover that one of the latter answer choices is actually *more* correct. Moreover, reading all of the answer choices can remind you of facts related to the question that can help you arrive at the correct answer. Sometimes, a misstatement or incorrect detail in one of the latter answer choices will trigger your memory of the subject and will enable you to find the right answer. Failing to read all of the answer choices is like not reading all of the items on a restaurant menu: you might miss out on the perfect choice.

11. Spot the Hedges

One of the keys to success on multiple-choice tests is paying close attention to every word. This is never truer than with words like almost, most, some, and sometimes. These words are called "hedges" because they indicate that a statement is not totally true or not true in every place and time. An absolute statement will contain no hedges, but in many subjects, the answers are not always straightforward or absolute. There are always exceptions to the rules in these subjects. For this reason, you should favor those multiple-choice questions that contain hedging language. The presence of qualifying words indicates that the author is taking special care with his or her words, which is certainly important when composing the right answer. After all, there are many ways to be wrong, but there is only one way to be right! For this reason, it is wise to avoid answers that are absolute when taking a multiple-choice test. An absolute answer is one that says things are either all one way or all another. They often include words like *every*, *always*, *best*, and *never*. If you are taking a multiple-choice test in a subject that doesn't lend itself to absolute answers, be on your guard if you see any of these words.

12. Long Answers

In many subject areas, the answers are not simple. As already mentioned, the right answer often requires hedges. Another common feature of the answers to a complex or subjective question are qualifying clauses, which are groups of words that subtly modify the meaning of the sentence. If the question or answer choice describes a rule to which there are exceptions or the subject matter is complicated, ambiguous, or confusing, the correct answer will require many words in order to be expressed clearly and accurately. In essence, you should not be deterred by answer choices that seem excessively long. Oftentimes, the author of the text will not be able to write the correct answer without offering some qualifications and modifications. Your job is to read the answer choices thoroughly and completely and to select the one that most accurately and precisely answers the question.

13. Restating to Understand

Sometimes, a question on a multiple-choice test is difficult not because of what it asks but because of how it is written. If this is the case, restate the question or answer choice in different words. This process serves a couple of important purposes. First, it forces you to concentrate on the core of the question. In order to rephrase the question accurately, you have to understand it well. Rephrasing the question will concentrate your mind on the key words and ideas. Second, it will present the information to your mind in a fresh way. This process may trigger your memory and render some useful scrap of information picked up while studying.

14. True Statements

Sometimes an answer choice will be true in itself, but it does not answer the question. This is one of the main reasons why it is essential to read the question carefully and completely before proceeding to the answer choices. Too often, test takers skip ahead to the answer choices and look for true statements. Having found one of these, they are content to select it without reference to the question above. Obviously, this provides an easy way for test makers to play tricks. The savvy test taker will always read the entire question before turning to the answer choices. Then, having settled on a correct answer choice, he or she will refer to the original question and ensure that the selected answer is relevant. The mistake of choosing a correct-but-irrelevant answer choice is especially common on questions related to specific pieces of objective knowledge. A prepared test taker will have a wealth of factual knowledge at his or her disposal, and should not be careless in its application.

15. No Patterns

One of the more dangerous ideas that circulates about multiple-choice tests is that the correct answers tend to fall into patterns. These erroneous ideas range from a belief that B and C are the most common right answers, to the idea that an unprepared test-taker should answer "A-B-A-C-A-D-A-B-A." It cannot be emphasized enough that pattern-seeking of this type is exactly the WRONG way to approach a multiple-choice test. To begin with, it is highly unlikely that the test maker will plot the correct answers according to some predetermined pattern. The questions are scrambled and delivered in a random order. Furthermore, even if the test maker was following a pattern in the assignation of correct answers, there is no reason why the test taker would know which pattern he or she was using. Any attempt to discern a pattern in the answer choices is a waste of time and a distraction from the real work of taking the test. A test taker would be much better served by extra preparation before the test than by reliance on a pattern in the answers.

FREE DVD OFFER

Don't forget that doing well on your exam includes both understanding the test content and understanding how to use what you know to do well on the test. We offer a completely FREE Test Taking Tips DVD that covers world class test taking tips that you can use to be even more successful when you are taking your test.

All that we ask is that you email us your feedback about your study guide. To get your **FREE Test Taking Tips DVD**, email freedvd@studyguideteam.com with "FREE DVD" in the subject line and the following information in the body of the email:

- The title of your study guide.
- Your product rating on a scale of 1-5, with 5 being the highest rating.
- Your feedback about the study guide. What did you think of it?
- Your full name and shipping address to send your free DVD.

Introduction

Function of the Test

The Florida Standards Assessments (FSA) English Language Arts (ELA) for Grade 3 is a Common Core-based exam given in the state of Florida. The exam measures education progress and determines whether or not a student is qualified to move on to the next grade. This specific guide tests concepts third graders should have mastered by the end of the year. In the spring of 2019, 2,333 third graders took the FSA ELA Grade 3 exam.

Test Administration

The FSA ELA Grade 3 is offered every year for students in the third grade who are enrolled in Florida public schools. Each student's particular district or school will provide parents with the dates students will test; but, to give an idea, the testing window for Grade 3 ELA in 2018-2019 school year was April 1st through 12th of 2019. Students may not retake the same test given in an established test administration window due to already being exposed to the test. However, there may be retake opportunities available at different times of year depending on your school's policy.

All students with disabilities are able to participate in the FSA. See the FAQs on fsaassessments.org for more information about how to request accommodations.

Test Format

The FSA ELA Grade 3 exam is eighty minutes in length given in two sessions. Students in third grade will take the ELA portion of the exam on paper. The Grade 3 ELA includes content covering literature and informational text. More details are in the table below:

Category	Genre	Percentage
Key Ideas and Details	Literature /Informational	15–25%
Craft and Structure	Literature/Informational	25–35%
Integration of Knowledge and Ideas	Literature/Informational	20–30%
Language and Editing	Literature/Informational	15–25%

Scoring

For FSA ELA, both scale scores and performance levels are reported. Scale scores determine five different performance levels that students may receive. Students may receive the following performance levels:

- Level 1: Inadequate (240–284)
- Level 2: Below satisfactory (285–299)
- Level 3: Satisfactory (300–314)
- Level 4: Proficient (315–329)
- Level 5: Mastery (330–360)

Beside each performance level above is also the scale score which determines the placement level. Scaled scores for grade 3 are between 240 and 360.

Recent/Future Developments

The FSA replaced the FCAT in 2014 as the state-wide standardized test used in Florida public schools.

Literature

Summarizing a Complex Text

A **summary** is a paragraph written about a story. A summary is written by the reader in their own words. To summarize a story, students should know the major points of the story. It may be helpful to outline the story to get a big picture view of it. Students should ignore small details when they are summarizing a story. For example, a summary wouldn't need to include a detail like the date or time, but it should talk about what the whole story is about. Students should use their own words when writing a summary.

Key Ideas and Details

The **main idea** of a story is what the story is about. To find the main idea, students should ask these questions: "What's the point? What does the author want us to learn?" Everything in the story should point back to the main idea. When you read a story, you will find the main idea in the beginning of the story.

Details are things that develop the main idea. Details make up the bulk of the story. Without supporting details, the main idea would simply be a statement. Lots of details are needed to give the main idea truth. Details can often be found by recognizing the key words that introduce them. The following example offers several supporting details, with key words underlined:

> Do you want to vacation at a Caribbean island destination? We chose to go to St. Lucia, and it was the best vacation we ever had. We lounged in crystal blue waters, swam with dolphins, and enjoyed a family-friendly resort and activities. One of the <u>first</u> activities we did was free diving in the ocean. We put our snorkels on, waded into the ocean, and swam down to the ocean floor. The water was clear all the way down—the greens and blues were so beautiful. We saw a stingray, some conches, and a Caribbean Reef Shark. The shark was so scary, I came up to the surface after that! <u>Another</u> activity we did was lying on the beach. We just relaxed and watched the warm sun baking the sand and the water. <u>Finally</u>, our activities concluded in getting massages and watching other kids play with a Frisbee in front of the water.

The underlined words are the key words that show what the details are. The details can be summarized as follows:

- We free dove in the ocean.
- We enjoyed lying on the beach.
- We got massages and watched other kids play with a Frisbee.

The details show that the main idea is going to St. Lucia for the "best vacation we ever had."

Details are more specific than the main idea. Even so, they should be directly related to the main idea. Without good supporting details, the writer's main idea will be too weak.

Types of Fiction and Characters

Fiction can be broken down into **fiction genres**—types of fiction. Some of the more common genres of fiction are as follows:

- **Classical fiction**: A work of fiction considered timeless in its message or theme, remaining meaningful for a long period of time. An example is Charlotte Brontë's *Jane Eyre* or Mark Twain's *Adventures of Huckleberry Finn*

- **Fables**: Short fiction that generally features animals, fantastic creatures, or other forces within nature. These characters will have human-like characteristics. Fables have a moral lesson for the reader. An example of a collection of fables is *Aesop's Fables*.

- **Fairy tales**: Children's stories with magical characters in imaginary, enchanted lands. Fairytales show a struggle between good and evil. Examples of fairy tales are Hans Christian Anderson's *The Little Mermaid* and *Cinderella* by the Brothers Grimm.

- **Fantasy**: Fiction with magic that cannot happen in the real world. Sometimes includes some form of sorcery or witchcraft and sometimes set in a different world. Examples are J.R.R. Tolkien's *The Hobbit*, J.K. Rowling's *Harry Potter and the Sorcerer's Stone*, and George R.R. Martin's *A Game of Thrones*.

- **Folklore**: Types of fiction passed down from oral tradition. Folklore can also be stories native to a particular region or culture. They are designed to help humans cope with their condition in life and validate traditions and beliefs. Examples of folklore is William Laughead's *Paul Bunyan and The Blue Ox*, or the Buddhist story of "The Banyan Deer."

- **Mythology**: Closely related to folklore but more widespread. Myths feature mystical, otherworldly characters. It addresses the basic question of why and how humans exist. In many myths, there are gods or heroes captured in some sort of struggle. Examples are Greek myths, Genesis I and II in the Bible, and Arthurian legends.

- **Science fiction**: Fiction that involves futuristic or otherworldly events involving time travel, space, technology, or fictional worlds. Some examples are *The Giver* by Lois Lowry, *Ender's Game* by Orson Scott Card, *The City of Ember* by Jeanne DuPrau, or *The Little Prince* by Antoine de Saint-Exupery

- **Short stories**: Short works of fiction with fully-developed themes and characters, focused on mood, generally developed with a single plot. Examples are Edgar Allan Poe's "Fall of the House of Usher," Shirley Jackson's "The Lottery," or Isaac Bashevis Singer's "Gimpel the Fool"

Characters are the people inside the story you are reading. **Major** characters are important to the story because the plot cannot go on without them. A major character can be considered a **hero**, also called a **protagonist**. An example of a hero is Wonder Woman or Superman. Sometimes major characters might also be called an antagonist. **Antagonists** usually fight against the protagonist. They are the bad guys. An example of an antagonist is Voldemort from *Harry Potter* or the Joker from the comic book series.

Dynamic characters are characters that change a lot throughout the story. **Static** characters do not change at all. A **flat** character is one that does not have a lot of depth, which means they are shallow or predictable. A **rounded** character, on the other hand, has a lot of depth, which means they learn a lot throughout the story. Sometimes the narrator of a story or the speaker in a poem can be a character.

Craft and Structure

Literal and Nonliteral Language

Literal language is the dictionary definition of a word or phrase. **Nonliteral** language means that the words do not mean exactly as they are said. For example, if I said, "it's raining cats and dogs!" that is considered nonliteral language. This is because it cannot *literally* be raining cats and dogs. If I said, "Wow, it's raining really hard!" that is considered literal language, because the rain could be coming down on the earth really hard. In order to tell the difference between literal and nonliteral language, it's important to use **context clues**, which are clues in the writing around the word or phrase.

Drama

Drama is when actors perform and speak for a theater, the radio, or the television. Drama is made up of different scenes, dialogue, and characters who perform to move the action along. Drama in a theater has **stage directions**, which are instructions that tell the actors what to do. **Dialogue** is the words characters say to each other or the audience throughout the play. **Setting** in a drama is the time and place from which the story is told. In *Little Red Riding Hood*, the setting is in the woods at night. Sometimes dramas have a **script**, which is the text of a play. The actors use a **script** to learn about the drama and what they need to say as characters in that drama.

The list below talks about the different types of plays or dramas:

- **Comedy**: A play or drama that is funny. Comedies are used to make the audience laugh or to entertain them. The movie *Ice Age* is a comedy.

- **History**: A play or drama that tells a story about history. Many times, kings and queens are involved. Shakespeare wrote a lot of historical plays. Shakespeare's *King Richard III* and Arthur Miller's *The Crucible* are history plays.

- **Tragedy**: A serious drama that can be sad. Examples of tragedies are *Up*, *Bambi*, or *The Fox and the Hound.*

- **Melodrama**: A melodrama is a very dramatic, sensitive story. *Pride and Prejudice* is a very emotional melodrama.

- **Tragi-comedy**: A play or drama that can be both funny and sad at the same time. An example is *The Lion King*, which can make us either laugh or cry.

Poetry

Poetry is words and sentences made into lines and stanzas that has a unique focus on the rhythm of language. Poems can be emotional, funny, serious, smart, or silly. A poem is not an entire story, though it may tell one. Poetry can be considered a word picture for the reader.

Poems have been used throughout the years to make the audience feel something in their heart. Poetry uses figurative language and rhythm to create the effect of emotion. Nursery rhymes can be considered poems, because they have words broken into lines and stanzas, and they use rhyme and meter. Other poems don't rhyme at all but just use words to make a beautiful feeling come to life. A **stanza** in a poem is when there is a new block of poetry. It's kind of like a paragraph, but inside a poem. Below, count the stanzas. The poem should have five stanzas.

"The Fly" by William Blake

Little Fly
Thy summer's play,
My thoughtless hand
Has brush'd away.

Am not I
A fly like thee?
Or art not thou
A man like me?

For I dance
And drink & sing;
Till some blind hand
Shall brush my wing.

If thought is life
And strength & breath;
And the want
Of thought is death;

Then am I
A happy fly,
If I live,
Or if I die.

Notice also the **rhymes** in the poem. Rhymes are when word-endings sound the same. "Breath" and "death" is a rhyme. "Sing" and "wing" is a rhyme." "Play" and "away" is a rhyme.

The following chart discusses different types of poems:

Type	Poetic Structure	Example
Ballad	A poem or song passed down orally which tells a story and in English tradition usually uses an ABAB or ABCB rhyme scheme	William Butler Yeats' "The Ballad of Father O'Hart"
Epic	A long poem from ancient oral tradition which narrates the story of a hero	Homer's *The Odyssey* Virgil's *The Aeneid*
Haiku	A Japanese poem of three unrhymed lines with five, seven, and five syllables (in English) with nature as a common subject matter	Matsuo Bashō "An old silent pond . . . A frog jumps into the pond, splash! Silence again."
Limerick	A five-line poem written in an AABBA rhyme scheme, with a witty focus	From Edward Lear's *Book of Nonsense*: "There was a Young Person of Smyrna Whose grandmother threatened to burn her . . ."
Ode	A formal lyric poem that addresses and praises a person, place, thing, or idea	Edna St. Vincent Millay's "Ode to Silence"
Sonnet	A fourteen-line poem written in iambic pentameter	Shakespeare's Sonnets 18 and 130

Nonfiction
Nonfiction stories are stories that are true. They are about real-life events. Fiction is made-up stories, and nonfiction is real stories. There are several common types of literary non-fiction:

Biography
A **biography** is a story written about a real person. It has true details of the person's life. Stories that tell about a person's life must be well-researched so the authors can get the facts right. The sources the writer uses to get their facts must be reliable too. A biography reflects the time and place in which the person lived. The goal of a biography is so that we can understand the person's real-life experience. Examples of biographies include *Amelia Lost* by Candace Fleming and *A Splash of Red* by Jennifer Bryant.

Autobiography
An **autobiography** is about a real-life person written by themselves. For example, let's say your name was Eliza Smith. If you wanted to write a story about yourself, called *The Life of Eliza Smith*, you would be writing an autobiography. An autobiography will be told in first person, which uses the words "I, me, my, myself." Examples of autobiographies include *Night* by Elie Wiesel and *Margaret Thatcher: The Autobiography* by Margaret Thatcher.

Memoir
A **memoir** is a story of a person's life written by someone who has personal, intimate knowledge of the information. Memoir, autobiography, and biography are very similar, but a memoir covers a specific timeline of events. For example, a memoir might cover details of a person's childhood. It is also less formal and tends to focus on the emotional aspect of the presented timeline of events. Some examples

of memoirs in literature include *Angela's Ashes* by Frank McCourt and *All Creatures Great and Small* by James Herriot.

Journalism
Journalism writing is travel writing, nature writing, sports writing, the interview, and the essay. Some examples include Elizabeth Kolbert's "The Lost World," in the Annals of Extinction series for *The New Yorker* and Gary Smith's "Ali and His Entourage" for *Sports Illustrated*.

Author's Purpose
When writers create stories, sometimes they have their own viewpoint. It's important for readers to develop their own viewpoint different from the writer. No matter how true a story may seem, sometimes the writer exaggerates so readers will enjoy the story more. This means that not every detail of every story is true. Sometimes the author's opinion might be different from your own opinion. That's okay too. See what the author has to say about their opinion and if it changes your mind or not.

Sometimes the author also has a **purpose** to their writing. An author's purpose might be to make you laugh. An author's purpose might be to inform you on how to make a sandwich. You can probably tell what an author's purpose is at the very beginning of every story. There are four purposes of writing: to inform, to persuade, to describe, and to entertain. Informative writings tell us about things we don't already know about. Persuasive writing is writing that tries to make you act or think in a certain way. Descriptive writing is designed to paint a picture in your mind, while writings that entertain are stories that are fun, scary, or dramatic.

Inferring a Conclusion
An **inference** means drawing a conclusion about a story that isn't stated directly in the story. For example, what conclusion can you infer from the sentences below?

> Lindsay, covered in flour, moved around the kitchen frantically. Her mom yelled from another room, "Lindsay, we're going to be late!

You can conclude that Lindsay's next steps are to finish baking, clean herself up, and head off somewhere with her baked goods. Notice that the conclusion may not be true, but it probably is. Many conclusions are not apparent in the story, so they have to be drawn out by the reader.

Figurative Language

Figurative language paints a picture for the reader through words. Figurative language is like saying "Your eyes are blue as the ocean" or "I can jump higher than a sky scraper!" None of these phrases are literally true, but they point out *how* blue or *how* high something is. Figurative language is the *fun* part of language because you can be creative! Some examples of figurative language are in the following table:

	Definition	Example
Simile	Compares two things using "like" or "as"	Her hair was like gold.
Metaphor	Compares two things as if they are the same	He was a giant teddy bear.
Idiom	Using words with predictable meanings to create a phrase with a different meaning	The world is your oyster.
Alliteration	Repeating the same beginning sound or letter in a phrase for emphasis	The busy baby babbled.
Personification	Giving human characteristics to an object or an animal	The house glowered menacingly with a dark smile.
Foreshadowing	Giving an indication that something is going to happen later in the story	I wasn't aware at the time, but I would come to regret those words.
Symbolism	Using symbols to represent ideas and provide a different meaning	The ring represented the bond between us.
Onomatopoeia	Using words that imitate sound	The tire went off with a bang and a crunch.
Imagery	Using sight words to make the images jump out of a story and into your senses	The sky was painted with red and pink and streaked with orange.
Hyperbole	Using exaggeration not meant to be taken literally	The puppy weighed less than a feather.

Effect of Word Choice

The author creates their story through words, so their **word choice** is important. The words an author chooses might be to bring out a certain mood from the audience. Or it may be because the author is trying to do something special with words that no one else has done before. Word choice is very important to a story because words make us feel a certain way toward the characters, the story, and the author.

Major Literary Works and Authors

The following chart offers some examples of popular stories, but the list not exhaustive.

<u>American</u>
Fictional Prose
      Harriet Beecher Stowe | *Uncle Tom's Cabin*
      Ernest Hemingway | *For Whom the Bell Tolls*
      Jack London | *The Call of the Wild*
      Toni Morrison | *Beloved*
      N. Scott Momaday | *The Way to Rainy Mountain*
      J.D. Salinger | *Catcher in the Rye*
      John Steinbeck | *Grapes of Wrath*
      Alice Walker | *The Color Purple*
Drama
      Edward Albee | *Who's Afraid of Virginia Woolf?*
      Lorraine Hansberry | *A Raisin in the Sun*
      Amiri Baraka | *Dutchman*
      Eugene O'Neill |*Long Day's Journey into Night*
      Sam Shephard | *Buried Child*
      Thornton Wilder I *Our Town*
      Tennessee Williams | *A Streetcar Named Desire*
Poetry
      Anne Bradstreet | "In Reference to her Children, 23 June 1659"
      Emily Dickinson | "Because I could not stop for Death"
      Sylvia Plath | "Mirror"
      Langston Hughes | "Harlem"
      Edgar Allen Poe | "The Raven"
      Phillis Wheatley | "On Being Brought from Africa to America"
      Walt Whitman | "Song of Myself"
Literary Non-fiction
      Maya Angelou | *I Know Why the Caged Bird Sings*
      Truman | *Capote In Cold Blood*
      Frederick Douglass | *My Bondage and My Freedom*
      Archie Fire | *Lame Deer The Gift of Power: The Life and Teachings of a Lakota Medicine Man*
      Helen Keller | *The Story of My Life*
      Dave Pelzer | *A Child Called "It"*

<u>British</u>
Fictional Prose
      John Bunyan | *The Pilgrim's Progress*
      Joseph Conrad | *Heart of Darkness*
      Charles Dickens | *Tale of Two Cities*
      George Eliot | *Middlemarch*
      George Orwell | *1984*
      Mary Shelley | *Frankenstein*

Drama

    Samuel Beckett | *Waiting for Godot*

    Caryl Churchill | *Top Girls*

    William Congreve | *The Way of the World*

    Michael Frayn | *Noises Off*

    William Shakespeare | *Macbeth*

    Oscar Wilde | *The Importance of Being Earnest*

Poetry

    Elizabeth Barrett Browning | "How Do I Love Thee? (Sonnet 43)"

    Robert Burns | "A Red, Red Rose"

    Samuel Taylor Coleridge | "Rime of the Ancient Mariner"

    T.S. Eliot | "Love Song of J. Alfred Prufrock"

    John Milton | "Paradise Lost"

Literary Non-fiction

    Vera Brittain | *Testament of Youth*

    T. E. Lawrence | *Seven Pillars of Wisdom*

    Doris Lessing | *Going Home*

    Brian Blessed | *Absolute Pandemonium: The Autobiography*

    Virginia Woolf | *A Room of One's Own*

World

Fictional Prose

    Anonymous | *The Epic of Gilgamesh*

    Chinua Achebe | *Things Fall Apart*

    Margaret Atwood |*The Handmaid's Tale*

    Pearl S. Buck | *The Good Earth*

    Miguel de Cervantes |*Don Quixote*

    Fyodor Dostoyevsky | *Crime and Punishment*

    Gabriel Garcia Marquez | *One Hundred Years of Solitude*

    James Joyce | *Ulysses*

    Nikos Kazantzakis | *Zorba the Greek*

    Boris Pasternak | *Dr. Zhivago*

    Amy Tan | *The Joy Luck Club*

    Voltaire | *Candide*

Drama

    Bertolt Brecht | *Mother Courage and her Children*

    Anton Chekhov | *The Seagull*

    Lady Gregory | *Workhouse Ward*

    Henrik Ibsen | *A Doll's House*

    Luigi Pirandello | *Six Characters in Search of an Author*

    Molière | *Tartuffe*

    Sophocles | *Antigone*

    August Strindberg | *Miss Julie*

    Vyasa | *The Bhagavad Gita*

    Johann Wolfgang von Goethe |*Faust*

Poetry

Anonymous | *Beowulf*

Anonymous | *The Ramayana*

Dante Alighieri | *The Divine Comedy*

Federico García Lorca | *Gypsy Ballads*

Omar Khayyám | *The Rubaiyat*

Kahlil Gibran | *The Prophet*

Andrew Barton "Banjo" Paterson | *"Waltzing Matilda"*

Taslima Nasrin | *"Character"*

Kostis Palamas | *"Ancient Eternal And Immortal Spirit"*

Maria Elena Cruz Varela | *"Kaleidoscope"*

Unknown | The 23rd Psalm, the Judeo-Christian bible

Literary Non-fiction

Pavel Basinsky | *Flight from Paradise*

Jung Chang | *Wild Swans*

Confucius | *The Analects of Confucius*

Viktor Frankl | *Man's Search for Meaning*

Mahatma Gandhi | *India of my Dreams*

Nelson Mandela | *Long Walk to Freedom*

Fatema Mernissi | *Beyond the Veil*

Jonathan Swift | *"A Modest Proposal"*

Mythology

Homer | *The Iliad*

Homer | *The Odyssey*

Hesiod | *Theogony*

Ovid | *Metamorphoses*

Virgil | *Aeneid*

Valmiki | *Ramayana*

Vyasa | *Bhagavad Gita*

Epic of Gilgamesh

Ferdowsi | The Shahnameh

Beowulf

The Volsunga Saga

<u>Young Adult</u>

Fictional Prose

Jodi Lynn Anderson | *Tiger Lily*

Lois Lowry | *The Giver*

Scott O'Dell | *Island of the Blue Dolphins*

Katherine Paterson Jacob | *Have I Loved*

Antoine de Saint-Exupéry | *The Little Prince*

Ellen Raskin | *The Westing Game*

P. L. Travers | *Mary Poppins*

Marcus Zusak | *The Book Thief*

Drama

Peter Dee | *Voices from the High School*

William Gibson | *The Miracle Worker*

Poetry
    Sandra Cisneros | "Eleven"
    Eamon Grennan | "Cat Scat"
    Tom Junod | "My Mother Couldn't Cook"
    Tupac Shakur | "The Rose that Grew from Concrete"

Literary Non-fiction
    Sherman Alexie | *The Absolutely True Diary of a Part-Time Indian*
    Anne Frank | *The Diary of Anne Frank*
    Philip Hoose | *The Boys who Challenged Hitler*
    Cynthia Levinson | *We've Got a Job*
    Malala Yousafzai and Christina Lamb | *I am Malala*

Integration of Knowledge and Ideas

Theme or Central Message

The **theme** is the message of a story. For example, in a story about three girls who go to school together and who live down the road from one another, the theme might be the importance of friendship. Stories in fiction, drama, and poetry all have themes, whether it be love, friendship, family, courage, or trust. The theme of the story is conveyed through the characters' relationships with each other and their interactions with other characters, nature, or themselves.

The following themes are common in stories:

- Individual against the self—themes include pride, isolation, fulfillment, failure, internal struggles, or innocence.

- Individual against nature— themes include knowledge vs. ignorance, nature as beauty, quest for discovery, self-preservation, chaos and order, circle of life, death, and destruction of beauty

- Individual against society— themes include power, beauty, good, evil, war, role of men/women, wealth, corruption, change vs. tradition, heroism, or injustice

- Individual against another individual— relevant to themes of hope, loss of love or hope, sacrifice, power, revenge, betrayal, and honor

An example of a story with alternating themes is *How to Train Your Dragon*. The themes or messages in this story are Friendship, loving your enemies, and strength comes from within. *The Boxcar Children* has themes of family, the home, and resourcefulness.

How Authors Develop Theme

There are a lot of ways authors develop theme. They may compare or contrast characters, events, places, ideas, or historical settings. They may use analogies, metaphors, similes, allusions, or other literary devices to show the theme. An author's word choice and sentences can also show the theme. Authors will often develop themes through the development of characters, use of the setting, repetition of ideas, use of symbols, and through contrasting values. Authors, playwrights, and poets all develop themes in similar ways.

Authors often do research to contribute to the theme. In fiction and drama, this research may include historical information about the setting the author has chosen or include elements that make fictional characters, settings, and plots seem realistic to the reader. In nonfiction, research is very important since the information must be accurate. Nonfiction writing is true events that have happened in the past. In fiction, authors will add conflict in the story to help make a theme. This conflict may involve the storyline itself or may be trouble between the characters that needs to be solved. In nonfiction, this conflict may be a commentary on factual people and events.

Authors identify an audience for their writing, which is critical in shaping the theme of the work. For example, the audience for J.K. Rowling's *Harry Potter* series would be different than the audience for a biography of George Washington. The audience an author chooses to address is closely tied to the purpose of the work. The choice of an audience also drives the choice of language an author uses.

Plot

The **plot** is what happens in the story. Plots may contain only one problem, or they may contain lots of problems to be solved. All plots have a beginning, a rising action, a climax, a falling action, and a conclusion. The **conflict** moves the plot along and is something that the reader expects to be fixed by the end of the story.

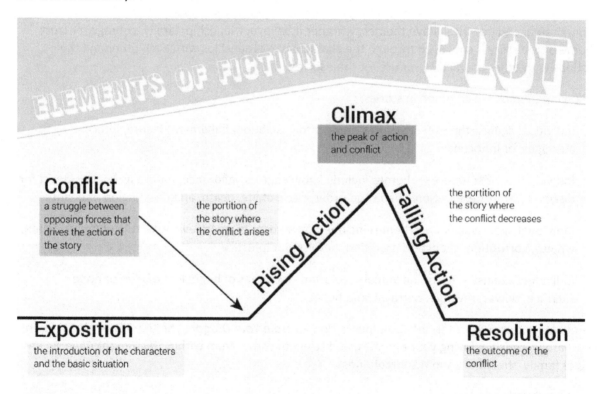

Tone

The **tone** of a story shows the author's attitude and opinion about the subject of the story. Tone can be expressed through word choice, imagery, figurative language, syntax, and other details. The emotion or mood the reader experiences relates back to the tone of the story. Some examples of possible tones are funny, sad, happy, angry, joyous, calm, or excited.

Setting

The **setting** is the time and place where the story occurs. It includes time or time span, places, climates, geography, or culture. The book *Harry Potter* has multiple settings. Sometimes the setting is at

Hogwarts, sometimes it is on Pivet Drive with Harry's aunt and uncle, and sometimes it is in Hogsmeade Village drinking butterbeer.

Foundational Skills

Phonics and Word Recognition

Phonics is the ability to look at letter-sounds to pronounce written words. Students with strong phonics skills can easily recognize familiar written words. Phonics allows young readers to translate printed words into recognizable speech. Practicing sounding out words is important as well as finding exceptions to the letter-sound relationships.

Morphology

By analyzing and understanding Latin, Greek, and Anglo-Saxon word roots, prefixes, and suffixes, one can better understand word meanings. Of course, people can always look words up if a dictionary or thesaurus if available but meaning can often be gleaned on the spot if the writer learns to dissect and examine words.

A word can consist of the following:

- root
- root + suffix
- prefix + root
- prefix + root + suffix

For example, if someone was unfamiliar with the word *submarine,* they could break the word into its parts.

- prefix + root
- sub + marine

It can be determined that *sub* means *below* as in *subway* and *subpar*. Additionally, students can see that *marine* refers to *the sea* as in *marine life*. Thus, it can be figured that *submarine* refers to something below the water.

Roots

Roots are the basic components of words. Many roots can stand alone as individual words, but others must be combined with a prefix or suffix to be a word. For example, *grad* is a root, but it needs a suffix to be an actual word (*graduate*).

Prefixes

A **prefix** is a word, letter, or number that is placed in front. It is often added to a root word to add a meaning to it. When written alone, prefixes are followed by a dash to show that the root word follows. Some of the most common prefixes are the following:

Prefix	Meaning	Example
dis-	not or opposite of	disabled
in-, im-, il-, ir-	not	illiterate
re-	again	return
un-	not	unpredictable
anti-	against	antibacterial
fore-	before	forefront
mis-	wrongly	misunderstand
non-	not	nonsense
over-	more than normal	overabundance
pre-	before	preheat
super-	above	superman

Suffixes

A **suffix** is a letter or group of letters added at the end of a word to form another word. The word created from the root word and suffix is either a different tense of the same root (*help + ed = helped*) or a new word (*help + ful = helpful*). When written alone, suffixes are preceded by a dash to indicate that the root word comes before.

Some of the most common prefixes are the following:

Suffix	Meaning	Example
Ed	makes a verb past tense	Wash*ed*
Ing	makes a verb a present participle verb	Wash*ing*
Ly	to make characteristic of	Love*ly*
s/es	to make more than one	chair*s*, box*es*
Able	can be done	Deplor*able*
Al	having characteristics of	Comic*al*
Est	comparative	Great*est*
Ful	full of	Wonder*ful*
Ism	belief in	Commun*ism*
Less	without	Faith*less*
Ment	action or process	Accomplish*ment*
Ness	state of	Happi*ness*
ize, ise	to render, to make	steri*lize*, adver*tise*
cede/ceed/sede	go	concede, proceed, supersede

Here are some helpful tips:

- When adding a suffix that starts with a vowel (for example, -ed) to a one-syllable root whose vowel has a short sound and ends in a consonant (for example, *stun*), double the final consonant of the root (*n*).

    stun + ed = stun*n*ed

    Exception: If the past tense verb ends in *x* such as *box*, do not double the *x*.

    box + ed = boxed

- If adding a suffix that starts with a vowel (-*er*) to a multi-syllable word ending in a consonant (*begin*), double the consonant (*n*).

    begin + er = begin*n*er

- If a short vowel is followed by two or more consonants in a word such as *i+t+c+h = itch,* do <u>not</u> double the last consonant.

    itch + ed = itched

- If adding a suffix that starts with a vowel (-*ing*) to a word ending in *e* (for example, *name*), that word's final *e* is generally (but not always) dropped.

    name + ing = naming
    exception: manage + able = manag*e*able

- If adding a suffix that starts with a consonant (-*ness*) to a word ending in *e* (*complete*), the *e* generally (but not always) remains.

    complete + ness = completeness
    exception: judge + ment = judgment

- There is great diversity on handling words that end in *y*. For words ending in a vowel + *y*, nothing changes in the original word.

    play + ed = played

- For words ending in a consonant + *y*, change the *y* to *i* when adding any suffix except for –*ing*.

    marry + ed = married
    marry + ing = marrying

Fluency

<u>Reading with Accuracy and Fluency</u>
Students should be able to read a third-grade text by themselves, reading each word at a rate of speed at which they can understand the meaning of the words. Students should not make any unnecessary pause between words in a sentence, paying attention to punctuation marks when reading. If there is a

24

period at the end of the sentence, a brief pause, or breath, is needed. If an exclamation mark is used, your voice should show excitement when reading the sentence.

Reading Text with Purpose and Understanding

It is important to decide why you are reading a text. **Informational** texts are written to inform readers about a topic. This means readers should learn something from reading. **Persuasive** texts are written to get readers to agree with an idea or to take some kind of action. You should be able to recognize the ideas that are being presented and decide whether you agree or not.

Understanding the plot in a short story is another key skill you will need. The **plot** of the story is the sequence of events that happens from the beginning to the end of the story. The plot begins with the setting of the story. The **setting** is when and where the story takes place. There will be one or two main **characters** in a story that encounter some type of problem, or **conflict**. These characters will have to make a decision about how to resolve their problem, called the **resolution**, before the story ends. Think about the story, "Goldilocks and the Three Bears." The setting of the story is in a cabin in the woods. Goldilocks is the main character. Although Goldilocks tries the porridge, rocking chairs, and beds in the bears' house, her problem, or the conflict, is actually that the bears come home and find her. The resolution is that she gets scared and runs away from the bears.

Making inferences about a character is not always easy. Inferences are not always stated, and sometimes the reader has to infer or take an educated guess about what is happening. **Inferences** are conclusions that are based on the information you are given. First, think about what you have learned or know based on what you read. Let's pretend you are reading "The Three Little Pigs." You know that the story is about a Big Bad Wolf who comes to blow all of the pigs' houses down. What if I told you the Big Bad Wolf blew the first two houses down? Then we would infer that the first two houses were built with a weak material, like straw or paper. What if I told you the Big Bad Wolf could not blow the third house down? Then we would infer that the third house was built with a strong material, like stone or brick.

Reading Poetry

Students should read poetry out loud with accuracy, appropriate rate, and expression. When reading a poem, say the words correctly and at the speed you use when you talk. Just like other types of writing, read the lines without hesitating between words. Read with good expression in your voice and pay attention to punctuation marks. If you are reading a poem by yourself and you don't know what a word means, reread the line over and see if you can understand what the word means by its context. Or, you can go to a dictionary and look up the word there.

Poems have **stanzas**, which are short paragraphs inside a poem. Poems also have **rhyme scheme**, which is the rhyming pattern of the last word in each line of the poem. Rhyme schemes are labeled using letters of the alphabet. For example, ABAB, CDCD, EFEF, GG denotes the poem is a sonnet because it is fourteen lines with a couplet at the end. A couplet is two lines next to each other that have the same end rhyme.

Figurative Language

Some popular figurative language used in text includes similes, metaphors, and idioms. A **simile** is a comparison of similar things using the words "like" or "as." Let's look at the following example of a simile:

Kroger sells apples as big as baseballs.

In this sentence, the size and shape of the apples is being compared to the size and shape of a baseball.

A **metaphor** is a comparison of unlike things and does NOT use the words "like" or "as." Let's look at the following example of a metaphor:

Marcy's room was a disaster area.

This sentence compares the messy state of Marcy's room to the disorganization of a disaster area.

Common idioms are also useful to know. An **idiom** is an expression that takes on a meaning different than what the words in the phrase actually mean. "In a pickle" is an idiom. The words suggest the phrase has something to do with an actual pickle, like you would put on your hamburger. However, the phrase means "in an awkward situation." It might be used like this:

I was in a pickle when my swim trunks fell down when I got out of the pool!

Informational Text

Key Ideas and Details

Main Idea and Supporting Details of Informational Text

When you read a story, the main idea is usually what the story is about. The supporting details are the part of the story that talk about the main idea. But how do we find the main idea? The main idea is what the author wants to say to you. Then, we want to find the supporting details. The details provide examples to help make a point. Supporting details can be quotes or analysis or facts about the main idea. You should look at the supporting details and see if they support the main idea. This is how a story "flows" or makes sense. The better the story flows, the better the author connected the details to the main idea. The picture below shows how the main idea is connected to the supporting details.

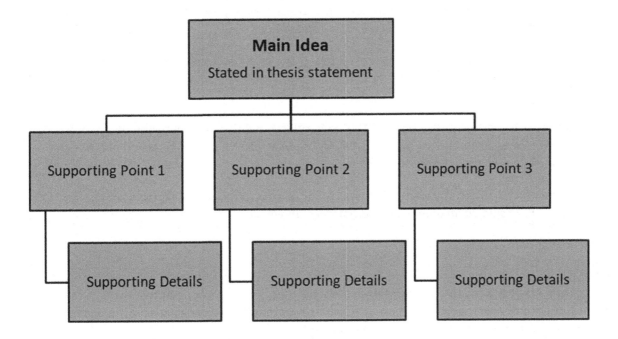

Transitions

Transitions are the glue that holds the writing together. They work to bring in new topics and supporting details in a smooth way. Usually, transitions are found at the start of a sentence. But they can also be located in the middle of a sentence to link words together.

Transition words connect clauses inside of sentences for smoother writing. "I dislike apples. They taste like garbage." is choppier than "I dislike apples because they taste like garbage." Transitions show us the relationship between ideas. They also allow for more complex sentence structures and can show the reader what kind of organization the author is using. For example, the use of the words *first, another*, and *finally* indicates that the writer will be listing the reasons why something happens.

The transition words below are put into different types. The different types show the relationships between ideas.

- General order: To elaborate on a point. Examples are *for example, for instance, to demonstrate, including, such as, in other words, that is, in fact, also, furthermore, likewise, and, truly, so, surely, certainly, obviously, doubtless*

- Chronological order: Going in the natural order of events. Examples are *before, after, first, while, soon, shortly thereafter, meanwhile*

- Numerical order/order of importance: Describing things in sequence or in order of importance. Examples are *first, second, also, finally, another, in addition, equally important, less importantly, most significantly, the main reason, last but not least*

- Spatial order: Talking about where something is located. Examples are *inside, outside, above, below, within, close, under, over, far, next to, adjacent to*

- Cause and effect order: When ideas are related to one another through cause and effect. Examples are *thus, therefore, since, resulted in, for this reason, as a result, consequently, hence, for, so*

- Compare and contrast order: Showing the similarities and differences between two or more objects or ideas. Examples are *like, as, similarly, equally, just as, unlike, however, but, although, conversely, on the other hand, on the contrary*

- Summary order: When you want to summarize or wrap up a thought. Examples are *in conclusion, to sum up, in other words, ultimately, above all*

Craft and Structure

<u>Word Phrases</u>
Sometimes you may be asked to identify clichés, literal phrases, and nonliteral phrases within a text. A cliché is a worn-out phrase that has been used so many times that it doesn't really have any meaning or significance today. The following sentence is an example of a cliché:

The diamond she wore was crystal clear.

The phrase "crystal clear" means the diamond is so clear you can see through it, but "crystal clear" has become so used that we forget a "crystal" is a type of rock itself and is used figuratively in this phrase.

A literal phrase is one that expresses a realistic idea. A sentence such as "The grass is green," is a literal phrase because there are no comparisons being made; the green is literally green. However, a nonliteral phrase expresses an idea that is unrealistic. In the sentence, "I love you *to the moon and back*," the italicized portion is a nonliteral phrase because the person saying the phrase most likely has not been to the moon and back.

<u>Text Features and Search Tools</u>
Text features are words that stand out in a text, such as the title, bolded headings, and bolded words. Use these features to help you locate and mark specific information within the passage. If a question

asks, "Which heading helps readers find the instructions for the board game?" browse the bolded headings until you find the section where this information is located.

Key words are words within a text that the author bolds or underlines to signify that the reader should learn them. Many times, key words within a text are followed by short definitions.

Hyperlinks are words that you can click on a computer screen. They are words that take you to another webpage so you can learn their definition or learn more about the word or process.

Sidebars are additional text features that are often found paired with longer texts. The information in a sidebar provides further information on the topic or discusses a similar topic. A longer passage may discuss the danger of children talking to strangers. The sidebar may list important numbers children can call when they are in danger, such as the police, the fire department, or poison control.

Point of View
The **point of view** is how the narrator or speaker tells the story. In poetry, the narrator of the poem is called the **speaker**. For example, is the narrator or speaker using the words "I, you, or they"? Is the speaker telling the story from their own viewpoint? Are they telling the story from another person's viewpoint? Or are they addressing the reader as "you" in the story? All of these points of view have different names: first person, second person, and third person. Below are details about each of the different points of view.

First Person
The **first-person** point of view is when the writer uses the word "I" in the story. A lot of poems also use the word "I" if they are trying to get the reader to feel a lot of emotion and empathize with the speaker. A lot of fiction is also written in first person. An example is *The Hunger Games* by Suzanne Collins. The narrator saying "I" most of the time is the main character in the story. The narrator/main character will say "I did this" or "I did that" to move the story along and talk about what they did that day.

Second Person
The **second-person** point of view is when the writer uses the pronoun "you." When a narrator uses second person, it is like they are talking directly to you. Books like *The Monster at the End of This Book* or *If You Give a Mouse a Cookie* are written in second person. These books talk to the reader directly and give instructions or tell you what happens if you do a certain thing.

Third Person
Third-person point of view is when the writer uses pronouns such as *him, her*, or *them*. Third person is very common because it is easy for authors to use and for readers to read. There are two main types of third person used in telling stories. **Third-person omniscient** means the narrator knows everything, including the thoughts and actions of every character. In **third-person limited**, the narrator tells the story through one character's thoughts/feelings, usually the main character.

Integration of Knowledge and Ideas

Illustrations
Illustrations are graphics that represent important information discussed in a passage. Some common forms of illustrations are maps, photographs, charts/tables, and classified ads. Passages that include an illustration will require multiple steps in the reading process. First, read and understand the text, then find major points and important details.

If there are any illustrations, read and interpret the illustrations to determine why they were used and what information they provide. If a text discusses the amount of rainfall in the southern states, a graph might be provided to give readers a visual of the text information. If a text discusses a famous photographer in Italy, a copy of his or her work may be shown.

Finally, combine the information you gathered from the text and the illustration to draw conclusions, make generalizations, or infer something about the topic. From a text and a photograph, you may conclude that the photographer preferred to paint colorful subjects such as flowers.

Logical Sequence

The way authors put together a story is important. Sometimes authors put their stories in certain structures. For example, a sequence structure might be when the author is trying to describe something in order. A comparison-contrast structure is not good for describing something in order, but it is good for comparing apples and oranges, or comparing cats and dogs. It's the author's job to put the right information into the correct structure.

Readers should be familiar with the five main text structures:

1. **Sequence** structure is when the order of events goes in chronological order. For a story, sequence structure means the plot goes through its usual elements: beginning, rising action, climax, falling action, and conclusion. Readers are introduced to characters, setting, and conflict in the beginning. In the rising action, tension and suspense go up. The climax is the point of no return and the peak of the story. Tension goes down during the falling action. In the conclusion, problems are solved and the story ends.

2. In the **problem-solution** structure, authors talk about a problem and then find a solution. This form of writing is usually divided into two paragraphs. It can be found in informational texts. For example, cell phone, cable, and satellite providers use this structure in manuals to help customers fix their problems with products.

3. **Comparison-contrast** structure is when authors want to discuss similarities and differences between things or ideas. For example, you would use compare/contrast to talk about how apples and oranges are different, or how cats and dogs are different. A comparison-contrast essay organizes one paragraph based on similarities and another based on differences. Words such as *however, but*, and *nevertheless* help signal a contrast in ideas.

4. **Descriptive** writing is when the story has a lot of details in it about things you see, hear, taste, touch and smell. Good descriptive stories have just the right amount of details. The plot still moves along but the details paint a picture in your mind as it moves. Descriptive writing will show you what's in the story by drawing on your five senses. Here is an example of descriptive writing:

> The little kitten had fur as white as a cloud and her purring vibrated when you put your ear up to her chest. She rolled around when she was happy, and her rough tongue was like sandpaper when she licked you. Honey the kitten was the sweetest pet we ever had.

When the description of the cat talks about her fur being white as a cloud, you picture a white kitten. You also get the sandpaper feeling when the writer talks about her tongue. This is descriptive writing.

5. Passages that use the **cause and effect** structure are simply asking *why* by demonstrating some type of connection between ideas. Words such as *if, since, because, then*, or *consequently* indicate relationship. By switching the order of a complex sentence, the writer can rearrange the emphasis on

different clauses. Saying *If Sheryl is late, we'll miss the dance* is different from saying *We'll miss the dance if Sheryl is late*. One emphasizes Sheryl's tardiness while the other emphasizes missing the dance. Paragraphs can also be arranged in a cause and effect format. Since the format—before and after—is sequential, it is useful when authors wish to discuss the impact of choices. Researchers often apply this paragraph structure to the scientific method.

Two Texts on the Same Topic

Sometimes when you read two texts side by side, you can point out what is the same or what's different about them. Let's say there are two passages side by side. Both passages discuss Mary's and Emma's participation at school. Some common ideas might be that Mary and Emma both have good grades because they go to tutorials every week in the library, or their favorite class is math. Several differences might be found in the passages as well. Let's look at the following paragraph for differences:

> Mary is very good at sports and is a member of the tennis and volleyball team. Mary is also a member of the Spanish club. However, Emma does not know how to play any sports, so she is a member of the choir.

The last example highlights the differences between Mary and Emma. Can you tell what they are?

Range of Reading and Level of Text Complexity

You should be able to independently read grade-level informational texts and demonstrate your comprehension by identifying major points, defining vocabulary words, finding the main idea, arranging events in sequential order, and locating details. Some informational texts include the following:

Social Studies Text

Social studies texts can explain an important event in history, such as the signing of the Declaration of Independence or the Gold Rush in California. They might talk about a person who made an impact in history, such as Johnny Appleseed or Benjamin Franklin.

Science Text

A **science text** is written to explore a topic related to science. It might discuss a single topic, such as mammals, plants, or tornadoes. It could explain a scientific process, such as how the earth revolves around the sun or the life cycle of a frog. A science text might explain the results of an experiment, like what happens to water when it freezes.

Technical Text

Technical texts usually tell you how to do something, such as how to build a birdhouse. The text might even include a diagram, or picture, to show how each step should look.

Writing Standards

Text Types and Purposes

Writers use different text types to share their ideas. There are three important text types below: opinion pieces, informative writing, and narratives.

When you know what text type you are reading, it makes the information much easier to understand. Below are three different text types and what they mean:

1. When authors write **opinion** pieces, they are giving their own thoughts and ideas about someone else's story. The topic, stance, and argument are found at the beginning of the writing. The opinion piece will give examples from the story to back up the writer's opinion.

Let's think about an example of an opinion piece. Say that we read a story about a little girl who goes to school. One day she gets sick and stays home from school, but in the story, it seems like she is only pretending to be sick. If you were to write an opinion piece, you would start with your opinion on the story. Your opinion would be: 1) the little girl is not really sick! or 2) the little girl is really sick! This would be an opinion piece, because you are giving your own thoughts about what happened in the story.

2. **Informative** writing gives instructions or information to the reader. It does not tell a story like a narrative and is not arguing anything like persuasive writing. Expository writing might have directions for how to do a task. Or, it will simply give information about something.

Sequence words such as *first*, *second*, and *third*, or *in the first place*, *secondly*, and *lastly* are used in expository writing. Common examples of expository writing include a teacher's lessons, cookbook recipes, and repair manuals.

3. **Narrative** writing is when an author tells a story. Narratives must have characters. Characters will be anything in the story that thinks, acts, or talks like a human. Sometimes characters are animals or objects. For example, the toaster in *The Brave Little Toaster* is a character, even though it is also an object.

Narratives must also have a plot or a sequence of events. Plots have a beginning, rising action, falling action, and conclusion. But sometimes plots are different and start in the middle of things instead of in the beginning. When the narrative starts in the middle of the plot, we usually have flashbacks telling us what happened to lead up to this point.

In narratives, there must also be conflict. Conflict can be internal or external. Internal conflict is when the character is in turmoil in their mind or heart. External conflict is when a character is fighting with something outside of themselves, like nature, another person, or society.

Production and Distribution of Writing

Development of a Story
Almost every story has three primary parts: a beginning, middle, and end. But organization is different for every type of writing. Informative and opinion writing use an introduction, body, and conclusion, whereas narrative works use a series of events with conflict and a resolution.

The beginning of a story will usually state the main idea or purpose of the writing. For a narrative piece, the beginning is the section that acquaints the reader with the characters and setting. The main idea in narrative may be given at the beginning or end of the story, but much of the time it is at the beginning. In information writing and opinion pieces, the beginning will contain the author's purpose for writing and will state the main idea.

The middle of a story or essay is called the **body**. The body will have different structures. It will have cause and effect, problem/solution, compare/contrast, or chronological structure.

The ending of a story is the end or conclusion. A solid ending ties together loose ends, resolves the action, highlights the main points, or repeats the main idea. A conclusion makes sure that readers come away from a story understanding the author's main idea. The table below highlights the important parts of a story.

Structure	Argumentative/Informative	Narrative
Beginning	Introduction Purpose, main idea	Orientation Introduces characters, setting, necessary background
Middle	Body Supporting details, reasons and evidence	Events/Conflict Story's events that revolve around a central conflict
End	Conclusion Highlights main points, summarizes and paraphrases ideas, reiterates the main idea	Resolution The solving of the central conflict

Planning, Revising, and Editing
The POWER strategy helps all students to take ownership of the writing process by encouraging them to focus on what they are writing.

The POWER strategy is an acronym for the following:

- Prewriting or Planning
- Organizing
- Writing a first draft
- Evaluating the writing
- Revising and rewriting

Prewriting and Planning
During the Prewriting and Planning phase, you will consider the audience you are writing to. The audience is the person or people who are going to read your writing. Then you will put together information you want to include in the piece of writing.

Organizing
When you organize a story or paper, there are many options to choose from. Of course, every story or piece of writing will have an introduction and a conclusion. There is also a middle part, called a body.

Here are the most common ways to organize the body of a paper: story/narrative, informative, opinion, persuasive, compare and contrast, explanatory, and problem/solution.

Writing

In this step, students write a complete first draft of their story or paper. It may be helpful for beginning writers to work in small groups or pairs. Verbalizing their thoughts before writing them is also a helpful technique. It also helps to write down ideas before writing down any sentences. For example, if you're writing a story about a bear, you might want to do an outline first:

- Introduction (introduce the bear and its family)
- Body (tell the story of the bear)
- Conclusion (end the story with something the bear learns)

Evaluating

When you evaluate your work, it means you read back over it and make sure everything sounds okay. Are all the words spelled right? Are the periods and commas in the right place? Does your story flow from a beginning to an ending? Evaluating your story will make it better in the end for your audience.

Revising and Rewriting

Finally, you will make any changes you need to after evaluating your story. Maybe you have to correct a misspelled word. Maybe you have to add a detail that wasn't there before. You will revise your writing until it is a final document and ready to be published or shown to the audience.

Using Technology to Produce and Publish Writing

Using technology such as computers and iPads can be useful to produce and publish writing, such as an essay, news article, personal letter, or research paper. Learning how to use the keyboard properly will also help you type quicker and get your ideas on the paper faster, so you don't lose track of them. The great thing about using a computer to produce and publish writing is that you can format the writing any way you want with tools such as margins, spacing, titles, and page numbers.

It is common to begin the writing process by brainstorming ideas about a topic. A rough draft is then written to form more complete ideas on a topic. The rough draft is then revised. Revisions are made to further improve organization and delete or add important information or details. Often, part of the revision process is sharing or expanding on ideas in small groups or with a partner. Edit the rough draft to demonstrate knowledge of correct grammar, spelling, and punctuation. Publishing a final draft is the last step in the process.

Research to Build and Present Knowledge

Conduct Research Projects

Research is meant is to provide an answer to an unknown question. For this reason, all good research papers state the topic in the form of a question. Then they seek to answer that question with clear ideas, arguments, and supporting evidence.

A **research question** is the primary focus of the research paper. The question should be based on a unique topic. To formulate a research question, you should begin by choosing a general topic of interest. Then, do some research where you can find out more information on that topic. This helps to narrow the topic into something original. The following question is an example of a research question, although it might be too general for a paper:

> What is most people's favorite kind of animal?

This research question might be too general. There are lots of people in the world! How will we ever know who *everyone's* favorite animal is? Maybe we should try narrowing down the topic. To narrow it down, the question could consider a specific population:

> What is the favorite animal of people in Ecuador?

This question is better. However, it does not address exactly why this research is being conducted or why anyone would care about the answer. Here's another possibility:

> What is the favorite animal of people in Ecuador and what does the answer say about how old they are?

This question is extremely specific and gives a very clear direction of where the paper is going. But sometimes the research question can be *too* specific. It's okay to change your question so that you can easily gather the facts you need. For example, you can see what the favorite animal is in South America instead of Ecuador, that way you have a much general scope of where to look.

Gathering Information

Relevant information is information that is important to the research question. When doing research online, it is easy to get overwhelmed with the amount of information. Before conducting research, then, remember to begin with a clear idea of the question you want answered.

For example, a student may be interested in learning more about why cows eat grass. If that student types "cows" into a search engine, he or she will have to sift through thousands of sites before finding anything related to that topic. But typing "why cows eat grass" will bring up relevant information to your topic. Being more specific is a good thing if you are getting too many results!

When using a book, students can look at the table of contents, glossary, or index to see whether the book contains relevant information before using it. If the student finds a big book about cows, he or she can flip to the index in the back, look for the word *food,* and find out how many references are listed in the book. If there are few or no references to the subject, it is probably not a good source.

When using research articles online, students may also consult the title, abstract, and keywords before reading the whole article. Referring to the date of publication will also determine whether the research contains up-to-date discoveries, theories, and ideas about the subject or is outdated.

The following questions will help determine whether a source is credible:

- Who is the author?
- What does the author do for a living?
- Does this person have experience with the topic?
- Is the author employed by any particular organization or sponsor?
- Does the author have any other books?
- Who published the work? Is it a well-known journal, like *National Geographic*, or a tabloid, like *The National Enquirer*?

- Is the publisher from a scholarly, commercial, or government association?
- Have they published other works?
- If a digital source, what kind of website hosts the text? Does it end in .edu, .org, or .com?
- Is there any bias in the writing?
- Is the writing factual or emotional?
- Does the work include diverse opinions or perspectives?
- Does the source contain any advertising?
- Are there any references?
- Are the references credible?
- Are the references from a related field?
- Are all of the conclusions, supporting details, or ideas backed with evidence?
- If a digital source, is it free of grammatical errors, poor spelling, and improper English?
- Do other published individuals have similar findings?
- Is the topic addressed throughout the writing?
- Does the work add new information to its topic?
- Does the writing target the audience appropriately?

Range of Writing

Writing Over Long and Short Time Frames

Being able to write compositions about a specific task, such as school dress code, ways to help the environment, or how to bake a cake, is a valuable skill. Works should be written with a clear purpose in mind, whether to inform, to persuade, or to entertain the readers, and using language appropriate for the reading audience.

You should be able to write compositions that require multiple steps and writing sessions to complete. The time frame for writing will vary based on individual teacher assignments, but usually this process is spread out over multiple days or weeks. Here are some steps of the research process:

- Research a topic and organize the information
- Create a rough draft based on the information found during research
- Reflect on the essay, thinking about the organization and/or information that could be added to better explain the points
- Make revisions to the composition, looking for errors in spelling, grammar, capitalization, punctuation, word use, verb tense, and sentence structure, to create a polished work as the final step of this process

A research paper can take a lot of time, whereas composing shorter works can be done more quickly in one or two writing sessions. For example, your teacher might ask you to write a one-page response to a story, a letter to a friend, or an explanation of how to make a sandwich.

Speaking and Listening

Comprehension and Collaboration

<u>Collaborative Discussions</u>
Classroom and small group discussions are a very popular way to learn about a topic. You will work in groups with students who are quick to learn the topic, and you will work in groups with students who struggle to understand the topic. Even though everyone has their own pace of learning, everyone in the group has an opinion that deserves to be heard.

Reading or studying assigned materials is an easy way to be prepared for classroom discussions. Use your knowledge of the topic to add ideas to discussions, ask questions, or present solutions.

Remember to be courteous while participating in group discussions. Such courtesies include listening to others' ideas carefully and being respectful of each participant's ideas and contributions. Stay focused on the topic so others aren't distracted. Use your knowledge to build on others' comments or ask valid questions. Take turns when speaking and avoid interrupting another participant. If you disagree with someone's opinion, do so politely. Argue your position with the understanding that not everyone will agree with you.

<u>Oral and Visual Presentation of Writing</u>
Visually means things you can see. Orally means things you can hear. Quantitatively means things you see on graphs or tables that involve numbers. Sometimes when we hear things out loud it can be difficult to know what their main idea is. But information shown to us or spoken out loud has a main idea just like any other information.

Any information you hear or see should have a clear beginning, middle, and end. Organization always makes any work more clear, concise, and logical. For a presentation, speakers should choose a primary topic and then discuss it in the following format:

- Introduce the main topic
- Provide evidence, supporting details, further explanation of the topic in the main body
- Conclude with a firm resolution and repetition of the main point

The beginning, middle, and end should also have effective transitions that make the presentation flow well. For example, a presentation should always begin with an introduction by the speaker, including what they do and what they are there to present. Good transitional introductions may begin with statements such as, *For those who do not know me, my name is...*, *As many of you know, I am...* or *Good morning everyone, my name is* ___. A good introduction grabs the attention of the audience.

After an introduction has been made, the speaker will then want to state the purpose of the presentation with a natural transition, such as *I am here to discuss...* or *This afternoon, I would like to present...*. Once the purpose has been identified, the speaker will want to stick to the main idea. The presenter should be certain to keep the main idea to one sentence. Sometimes too much information can confuse an audience. An introduction should be short and to the point.

If the presentation is a visual aid, supporting details should be presented in bullet points or lists. Good transitions such as *Let's begin with...* or *Now to look at...* make the presentation flow smoothly and logically. Keep the material short! This is extremely important in a presentation. Visual aids should be used only to emphasize points or explain ideas. All the supporting information should relate back to the main idea.

Finally, in the conclusion you should talk about the main point of the presentation again. The conclusion can inspire listeners to act or restate the most important points made in the speech. Speakers should also say "thank you" to the audience and ask if there are any questions.

<u>Evaluating a Speaker</u>
Evaluating a speaker is a lot like evaluating a story. A main difference is that you *hear* a speaker and you *read* a story. What are some of the things that stay the same?

Think about the speaker's stance on their position. For example, if they are talking about going on a vacation, where are they trying to persuade the audience to go? What is their purpose for talking about vacations?

A speaker may also use evidence to support their point. What kind of evidence is the speaker using? Are they using sources from the internet? Did they bring pictures in from their own vacation? What are some of the details they are using to get you to believe what they are saying?

Another important thing to pay attention to in a speech is word choice. Word choice says a lot about a speaker. Are they using big words or easy words? Are they passionate or are they neutral?

Tone and tone of voice can also influence the speaker's message. Students should be able to recognize different tones such as humor or sadness in a speaker.

When a speaker asks any questions to the audience, you should answer them! If the speaker asks if you understand everything but there's something you don't understand, speak up!

Asking questions to the speaker is really helpful too. When the speaker is done with their speech, asking them questions will make them feel like what they said matters. It will also help you to clear up anything you want to know that you didn't understand in the speech.

Presentation of Knowledge and Ideas

<u>Reporting on a Topic</u>
Giving a speech means that you will have people listening in your audience. If you are speaking in front of an audience, there are a few important things you should know.

You should use organization so the speech is easy to follow. You should also be able to present facts and research that shows your own perspective on the subject matter. For example, you should look up facts from credible sources but then explain why you think the facts are correct.

Always know your audience and purpose before planning a speech. As you think about what details you want to share, ask yourself if your audience will like these details. Provide fun and interesting details so that your audience won't be bored!

Finally, you should speak clearly so that your listeners can hear you. You should also speak slowly so that your listeners can follow along easily and so they won't have too many questions at the end.

Reading Clearly and Visual Aids

When you are speaking or reading to your audience it's important to speak clearly where your readers can understand you. If you are reading off a paper or out of a book, make sure you read at the right pace. If you read too fast, your audience will get confused, and if you read too slow, your audience will get frustrated. Read at a pace similar to how you speak.

Visual aids and audio recordings are really fun things to use in your speech! We'll talk about some media below that will help you add to your presentation so that your audience is entertained:

Microsoft PowerPoint is currently the most commonly used visual aid. You can use pictures, words, videos, and music to be presented on the same screen. It is just a projection of a computer screen onto the wall. You should use PowerPoint to help with your presentation, but you shouldn't use it for your *whole* presentation. This will make the audience bored. They want to hear what you have to say beyond the screen. Use fun pictures to add to the PowerPoint so that your audience will be entertained.

Handouts are a great way for the audience to feel more involved in a presentation. They can present lots of information that may be too much for a PowerPoint. They can also be taken home and reviewed later. The best handouts are those that do not contain all the information of a presentation but allow for the audience to take notes and complete the handout by listening or asking questions.

Whiteboards and **blackboards** are great for talking about hard concepts. This is because it allows the audience to follow along and copy down their own version of what is being written on the board. This visual aid is best used to explain concepts in mathematics and science.

Physical objects are a useful way to connect with the audience. It allows them to feel more involved. Because people interact with the physical world, physical objects can help students understand difficult ideas. Make sure you don't show the object you are talking about until you are ready to talk about it! If you show it too early, your audience might get distracted.

Videos are a great way to make a presentation fun by giving it sound, music, flow, and images. They are good for highlighting points, providing evidence for ideas, giving context, or setting tone. If you are doing a video, make sure it only lasts a minute or two so that you still have a chance to talk about your topic apart from the video.

Speaking and Presentation Skills

Similar to listening skills, students also need to be taught speaking and presenting skills. Students need to learn such skills as:

- How to introduce themselves
- How to make eye contact with listeners
- How to begin a conversation and keep it going
- How to interact with the audience
- How to answer questions
- How to have confidence
- How to ask for questions after

The following strategies can help teach speaking skills:

- You can help your student by asking open-ended questions. This helps them to answer a question in complete sentences without a "yes" or "no" answer.

- "I don't know" should not be accepted for an answer. Students should be taught that their thinking is valued rather than whether they *know* something.

- Teach your student how to take turns in the classroom fairly and to not interrupt one another.

- Students should be instructed not to read their presentations word for word, and to speak toward the audience instead of toward the project or PowerPoint slide.

- Videos of good and poor presentations can be shown as models for students to critique.

- Students should be taught to build in humor and good non-verbal communication into their presentations.

- Students should avoid repeating themselves or saying "um" or "like" too much.

Language

Cursive Skills

You need to be able to tell the difference between printed letters and cursive letters. You will be asked to identify the letters of the alphabet. For example, a cursive letter that looks like *a* is the printed letter "a." Not only is identifying letters important, but students should learn how to write their first and last names in cursive.

Conventions of Standard English

Parts of Speech
The English language has eight parts of speech, each serving a different grammatical function.

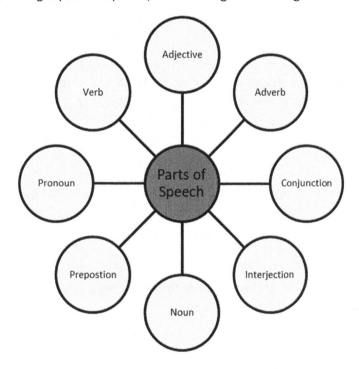

Verb
Verbs describe an action—e.g., *run*, *play*, *eat*—or a state of being—e.g., *is*, *are*, *was*. It is impossible to make a grammatically-complete sentence without a verb.

> He *runs* to the store.

> She *is* eight years old.

Noun
Nouns can be a person, place, or thing. They can refer to concrete objects—e.g., chair, apple, house—or abstract things—love, knowledge, friendliness.

> Look at the *dog*!

> Where are my *keys*?

Some nouns are countable, meaning they can be counted as separate entities—one chair, two chairs, three chairs. They can be either singular or plural. Other nouns, usually substances or concepts, are uncountable—e.g., air, information, wealth—and some nouns can be both countable and uncountable depending on how they are used.

> I bought three *dresses*.

> *Respect* is important to me.

> I ate way too much *food* last night.

> At the international festival, you can sample *foods* from around the world.

Proper nouns are the specific names of people, places, or things and are almost always capitalized.

> *Marie Curie* studied at the *Flying University* in *Warsaw, Poland*.

Pronoun

Pronouns are substitutes for nouns. Pronouns are often used to avoid constant repetition of a noun or to simplify sentences. **Personal pronouns** are used for people. Some pronouns are **subject pronouns**; they are used to replace the subject in a sentence—*I, we, he, she, they*.

> Is *he* your friend?

> *We* work together.

Object pronouns can function as the object of a sentence—me, us, him, her, them.

> Give the documents to *her*.

> Did you call *him* back yet?

Some pronouns can function as either the subject or the object—e.g., *you, it*. The subject of a sentence is the noun of the sentence that is doing or being something.

> *You* should try it.

> *It* tastes great.

Possessive pronouns indicate ownership. They can be used alone—*mine, yours, his, hers, theirs, ours*—or with a noun—*my, your, his, her, their, ours*. In the latter case, they function as a determiner, which is described in detail in the below section on adjectives.

> This table is *ours*.

> I can't find *my* phone!

Reflexive pronouns refer back to the person being spoken or written about. These pronouns end in -*self/-selves*.

I've heard that New York City is gorgeous in the autumn, but I've never seen it for *myself*.

After moving away from home, young people have to take care of *themselves*.

Indefinite pronouns are used for things that are unknown or unspecified. Some examples are *anybody, something,* and *everything.*

I'm looking for *someone* who knows how to fix computers.

I wanted to buy some shoes today, but I couldn't find *any* that I liked.

Adjective
An **adjective** modifies a noun, making it more precise or giving more information about it. Adjectives answer these questions: What kind? Which one?

I just bought a *red* car.

I don't like *cold* weather.

Adverb
Adverbs modify verbs, adjectives, and other adverbs. Words that end in –*ly* are usually adverbs. Adverbs answer these questions: *When? Where? In what manner? To what degree?*

She talks *quickly*.

The mountains are *incredibly* beautiful!

The students arrived *early*.

Please take your phone call *outside*.

Preposition
Prepositions show the relationship between different elements in a phrase or sentence and connect nouns or pronouns to other words in the sentence. Some examples of prepositions are words such as *after, at, behind, by, during, from, in, on, to,* and *with*.

Let's go *to* class.

Starry Night was painted *by* Vincent van Gogh *in* 1889.

Conjunction
Conjunctions join words, phrases, clauses, or sentences together, indicating the type of connection between these elements.

I like pizza, *and* I enjoy spaghetti.

I like to play baseball, *but* I'm allergic to mitts.

Coordinating conjunctions are short, simple words that can be remembered using the mnemonic FANBOYS: *for, and, nor, but, or, yet, so*. Other conjunctions are subordinating. **Subordinating** conjunctions introduce dependent clauses and include words such as *because, since, before, after, if,* and *while*.

Interjection
An **interjection** is a short word that shows greeting or emotion. Examples of interjections include *wow, ouch, hey, oops, alas,* and *hey.*

> *Wow*! Look at that sunset!

> Was it your birthday yesterday? *Oops*! I forgot.

Errors in Standard English Grammar, Usage, Syntax, and Mechanics
Sentence Fragments
A **complete sentence** requires a verb and a subject that expresses a complete thought. Sometimes, the subject is taken away in the case of the implied *you*, used in sentences that are the command or imperative form—e.g., "Look!" or "Give me that." It is understood that the subject of the command is *you*, the listener or reader, so it is possible to have a structure without a subject. Without these elements, though, the sentence is incomplete—it is a **sentence fragment**. While sentence fragments often occur in conversational English or creative writing, they are generally not appropriate in academic writing. Sentence fragments often occur when dependent clauses are not joined to an independent clause:

> *Sentence fragment*: Because the airline overbooked the flight.

The sentence above is a dependent clause that does not express a complete thought. What happened as a result of this cause? With the addition of an independent clause, this now becomes a complete sentence:

> Complete sentence: Because the airline overbooked the flight, several passengers were unable to board.

Sentences fragments may also occur through improper use of conjunctions:

> I'm going to the Bahamas for spring break. And to New York City for New Year's Eve.

While the first sentence above is a complete sentence, the second one is not because it is a prepositional phrase that lacks a subject [I] and a verb [am going]. Joining the two together with the coordinating conjunction forms one grammatically-correct sentence:

> I'm going to the Bahamas for spring break and to New York City for New Year's Eve.

Run-ons
A **run-on** is a sentence that is too long:

> This winter has been very cold some farmers have suffered damage to their crops.

The sentence above has two subject-verb combinations. The first is "this winter has been"; the second is "some farmers have suffered." However, they are simply stuck next to each other without any punctuation or conjunction. Therefore, the sentence is a run-on.

Another type of run-on occurs when writers use inappropriate punctuation:

> This winter has been very cold, some farmers have suffered damage to their crops.

Though a comma has been added, this sentence is still not correct. When a comma alone is used to join two independent clauses, it is known as a **comma splice**. Without an appropriate conjunction, a comma cannot join two independent clauses by itself.

Run-on sentences can be corrected by either dividing the independent clauses into two or more separate sentences or inserting appropriate conjunctions and/or punctuation. The run-on sentence can be amended by separating each subject-verb pair into its own sentence:

> This winter has been very cold. Some farmers have suffered damage to their crops.

The run-on can also be fixed by adding a comma and conjunction to join the two independent clauses with each other:

> This winter has been very cold, so some farmers have suffered damage to their crops.

Subject-Verb Agreement
In English, verbs must agree with the subject. The form of a verb may change depending on whether the subject is singular or plural, or whether it is first, second, or third person. For example, the verb *to be* has various forms:

> I <u>am</u> a student.
>
> You <u>are</u> a student.
>
> She <u>is</u> a student.
>
> We <u>are</u> students.
>
> They <u>are</u> students.

Errors occur when a verb does not agree with its subject. Sometimes, the error is readily apparent:

> We is hungry.

Is is not the appropriate form of *to be* when used with the third person plural *we*.

> We are hungry.

This sentence now has correct subject-verb agreement.

However, some cases are trickier, particularly when the subject consists of a lengthy noun phrase with many modifiers:

> Students who are hoping to accompany the anthropology department on its annual summer trip to Ecuador needs to sign up by March 31st.

The verb in this sentence is *needs*. However, its subject is not the noun adjacent to it—Ecuador. The subject is the noun at the beginning of the sentence—students. Because *students* is plural, *needs* is the incorrect verb form.

> *Students* who are hoping to accompany the anthropology department on its annual summer trip to Ecuador *need* to sign up by March 31st.

This sentence now uses correct agreement between *students* and *need*.

Another case to be aware of is a collective noun. A **collective noun** refers to a group of many things or people but can be singular in itself—e.g., *family, committee, army, pair team, council, jury*. Whether or not a collective noun uses a singular or plural verb depends on how the noun is being used. If the noun refers to the group performing a collective action as one unit, it should use a singular verb conjugation:

> The family is moving to a new neighborhood.

The whole family is moving together in unison, so the singular verb form *is* is appropriate here.

> The committee has made its decision.

The verb *has* and the possessive pronoun *its* both reflect the word *committee* as a singular noun in the sentence above; however, when a collective noun refers to the group as individuals, it can take a plural verb:

> The newlywed pair spend every moment together.

This sentence emphasizes the love between two people in a pair, so it can use the plural verb *spend*.

> The council are all newly elected members.

The sentence refers to the council in terms of its individual members and uses the plural verb *are*.

Overall though, American English is more likely to pair a collective noun with a singular verb, while British English is more likely to pair a collective noun with a plural verb.

Grammar, Usage, Syntax, and Mechanics Choices
Its and It's

These pronouns are some of the most confused in the English language as most possessives contain the suffix –'s. However, for *it*, it is the opposite. *Its* is a possessive pronoun:

> The government is reassessing *its* spending plan.

It's is a contraction of the words *it is*:

> *It's* snowing outside.

Saw and Seen

Saw and *seen* are both conjugations of the verb *to see*, but they express different verb tenses. *Saw* is used in the simple past tense. *Seen* is the past participle form of *to see* and can be used in all perfect tenses.

> I seen her yesterday.

46

This sentence is incorrect. Because it expresses a completed event from a specified point in time in the past, it should use simple past tense:

> I *saw* her yesterday.

This sentence uses the correct verb tense. Here's how the past participle is used correctly:

> I *have seen* her before.

The meaning in this sentence is slightly changed to indicate an event from an unspecific time in the past. In this case, present perfect is the appropriate verb tense to indicate an unspecified past experience. Present perfect conjugation is created by combining *to have* + past participle.

Then and Than
Then is generally used as an adverb indicating something that happened next in a sequence or as the result of a conditional situation:

> We parked the car and *then* walked to the restaurant.

> If enough people register for the event, *then* we can begin planning.

Than is a conjunction indicating comparison:

> This watch is more expensive *than* that one.

> The bus departed later *than* I expected.

They're, Their, and There
They're is a contraction of the words *they are*:

> *They're* moving to Ohio next week.

Their is a possessive pronoun:

> The baseball players are training for *their* upcoming season.

There can function as multiple parts of speech, but it is most commonly used as an adverb indicating a location:

> Let's go to the concert! Some great bands are playing *there*.

Insure and Ensure
These terms are both verbs. *Insure* means to guarantee something against loss, harm, or damage, usually through an insurance policy that offers monetary compensation:

> The robbers made off with her prized diamond necklace, but luckily it was *insured* for one million dollars.

Ensure means to make sure, to confirm, or to be certain:

> *Ensure* that you have your passport before entering the security checkpoint.

Accept and Except
Accept is a verb meaning to take or agree to something:

> I would like to *accept* your offer of employment.

Except is a preposition that indicates exclusion:

> I've been to every state in America *except* Hawaii.

Affect and Effect
Affect is a verb meaning to influence or to have an impact on something:

> The amount of rainfall during the growing season *affects* the flavor of wine produced from these grapes.

Effect can be used as either a noun or a verb. As a noun, *effect* is synonymous with a result:

> If we implement the changes, what will the *effect* be on our profits?

As a verb, *effect* means to bring about or to make happen:

> In just a few short months, the healthy committee has *effected* real change in school nutrition.

Structures of Sentences

All sentences contain the same basic elements: a subject and a verb. The **subject** is who or what the sentence is about; the **verb** describes the subject's action or condition. However, these elements, subjects and verbs, can be combined in different ways. The following graphic describes the different types of sentence structures.

Sentence Structure	Independent Clauses	Dependent Clauses
Simple	1	0
Compound	2 or more	0
Complex	1	1 or more
Compound-Complex	2 or more	1 or more

A **simple sentence** expresses a complete thought and consists of one subject and verb combination:

> The children ate pizza.

The subject is *children*. The verb is *ate*.

Either the subject or the verb may be **compound**—that is, it could have more than one element:

> *The children and their parents* ate pizza.

> The children *ate pizza and watched a movie.*

All of these are still simple sentences. Despite having either compound subjects or compound verbs, each sentence still has only one subject and verb combination.

Compound sentences combine two or more simple sentences to form one sentence that has multiple subject-verb combinations:

> *The children ate pizza,* and *their parents watched a movie.*

This structure is comprised of two independent clauses: (1) *the children ate pizza* and (2) *their parents watched a movie.* Compound sentences join different subject-verb combinations using a comma and a coordinating conjunction.

> I called my mom, *but* she didn't answer the phone.

> The weather was stormy, *so* we canceled our trip to the beach.

A **complex sentence** consists of an independent clause and one or more dependent clauses. Dependent clauses join a sentence using *subordinating conjunctions.* Some examples of subordinating conjunctions are *although, unless, as soon as, since, while, when, because, if,* and *before.*

> I missed class yesterday *because* my mother was ill.

> *Before* traveling to a new country, you need to exchange your money to the local currency.

The order of clauses determines their punctuation. If the dependent clause comes first, it should be separated from the independent clause with a comma. However, if the complex sentence consists of an independent clause followed by a dependent clause, then a comma is not always necessary.

A **compound-complex sentence** can be created by joining two or more independent clauses with at least one dependent clause:

> After the earthquake struck, thousands of homes were destroyed, and many families were left without a place to live.

The first independent clause in the compound structure includes a dependent clause—*after the earthquake struck.* Thus, the structure is both complex and compound.

Knowledge of Language

Root words, prefixes, and suffixes are an essential part of the English language. Let's break down the word *restocked. Stock* is the root word and can be used by itself in a sentence such as "Amanda's boss asked her to stock the shelves in the library." Re- is the prefix meaning "to do again." Use of the word restock might look like this: "Amanda's boss asked her to restock the shelves in the library with the books that had been returned." So, Amanda was asked to stock the shelves again. To change the word *restock* to past tense, add the suffix -ed to form the word *restocked.* The word *restocked* could be used in a sentence that says, "Amanda restocked the shelves on Friday before she left for vacation." There are many prefixes and suffixes that help change the meaning of a root word.

Students should learn how to use the dictionary to look up unfamiliar words. Dictionary skills include being able to alphabetize by locating a word using guide words, identifying the part of speech, determining correct pronunciation, and finding the correct definition if the word has multiple meanings.

There are many differences between spoken language and written language. It is important to understand the difference between **literal**, or realistic, phrases such as "Bob cut his finger to the bone" and **nonliteral**, or unrealistic, phrases such as "It was raining cats and dogs."

It's also important for students to be able to recognize words that show a character's feelings, such as happy, sad, and worried. Words like "frustrated," "aggravated," and "troubled" reveal a character's state of mind. A character's feelings and/or state of mind are sometimes directly stated in a text. An author might say, "Lucy was very aggravated at her brother for cutting her doll's hair." In this case, the author directly states that Lucy is aggravated and for what reason. However, some authors imply things about the character. This means that context clues are used to allow readers to make their own inferences about the character. For example, the author might write, "When she found her doll, Lucy's face turned red and she stomped downstairs waving her doll in her hand." In this case, the author doesn't specifically state that Lucy is very aggravated or angry, but readers can use the hints in the sentence to make an inference. Clues like "face turned red," "stomped downstairs," and "waving her doll in her hand" help the reader decide that Lucy was aggravated or angry.

Vocabulary Acquisition and Use

<u>Affixes</u>

Individual words are constructed from building blocks of meaning. An **affix** is an element that is added to a root or stem word that can change the word's meaning.

For example, the stem word *fix* is a verb meaning *to repair*. When the ending *–able* is added, it becomes the adjective *fixable*, meaning "capable of being repaired." Adding *un–* to the beginning changes the word to *unfixable*, meaning "incapable of being repaired." In this way, affixes attach to the word stem to create a new word and a new meaning. Knowledge of affixes can assist in deciphering the meaning of unfamiliar words.

A **prefix** is an affix attached to the beginning of a word. The meanings of English prefixes mainly come from Greek and Latin origins. The chart below contains a few of the most commonly used English prefixes.

Prefix	Meaning	Example
a-	not	amoral, asymptomatic
anti-	against	antidote, antifreeze
auto-	self	automobile, automatic
circum-	around	circumference, circumspect
co-, com-, con-	together	coworker, companion
contra-	against	contradict, contrary
de-	negation or reversal	deflate, deodorant
extra-	outside, beyond	extraterrestrial, extracurricular
in-, im-, il-, ir-	not	impossible, irregular
inter-	between	international, intervene
intra-	within	intramural, intranet
mis-	wrongly	mistake, misunderstand
mono-	one	monolith, monopoly
non-	not	nonpartisan, nonsense
pre-	before	preview, prediction
re-	again	review, renew
semi-	half	semicircle, semicolon
sub-	under	subway, submarine
super-	above	superhuman, superintendent
trans-	across, beyond, through	trans-Siberian, transform
un-	not	unwelcome, unfriendly

While the addition of a prefix alters the meaning of the base word, the addition of a **suffix** may also affect a word's part of speech. For example, adding a suffix can change the noun *material* into the verb *materialize* and back to a noun again in *materialization*.

Suffix	Part of Speech	Meaning	Example
-able, -ible	adjective	having the ability to	honorable, flexible
-acy, -cy	noun	state or quality	intimacy, dependency
-al, -ical	adjective	having the quality of	historical, tribal
-en	verb	to cause to become	strengthen, embolden
-er, -ier	adjective	comparative	happier, longer
-est, -iest	adjective	superlative	sunniest, hottest
-ess	noun	female	waitress, actress
-ful	adjective	full of, characterized by	beautiful, thankful
-fy, -ify	verb	to cause, to come to be	liquefy, intensify
-ism	noun	doctrine, belief, action	Communism, Buddhism
-ive, -ative, -itive	adjective	having the quality of	creative, innovative
-ize	verb	to convert into, to subject to	Americanize, dramatize
-less	adjective	without, missing	emotionless, hopeless
-ly	adverb	in the manner of	quickly, energetically
-ness	noun	quality or state	goodness, darkness
-ous, -ious, -eous	adjective	having the quality of	spontaneous, pious
-ship	noun	status or condition	partnership, ownership
-tion	noun	action or state	renovation, promotion
-y	adjective	characterized by	smoky, dreamy

Through knowledge of prefixes and suffixes, a student's vocabulary can be instantly expanded with an understanding of **etymology**—the origin of words. This, in turn, can be used to add sentence structure variety to academic writing.

Context Clues

When we know our affix, prefix, and suffix, it's easier to understand what words mean. However, some words are harder than others. In this case, rather than looking the word itself, it is useful to see what's around the word. This is called context. **Context** refers to the other words within the sentence that might help us figure out what the unknown word means. The following sentences shows the context for the word *spontaneous*.

> Rebecca had never been able to settle into a normal, boring life. Her *spontaneous* personality led her to quit a great job she had in Chicago. Instead, she moved to Mexico and lived in the beach.

Do you know what the word spontaneous means? If not, let's look at the surrounding words, or the **context**. The passage says that Rebecca did *not* live a normal life and did *not* live a boring life, so maybe spontaneous means abnormal or exciting. That's close! Spontaneous means doing something that you haven't planned out. If you have a spontaneous personality, that means you might do exciting things on a whim. If she quit a good job she had, it may also mean that she does things quickly without thinking. The word spontaneous also indicates someone who may not think things through.

Context clues are also helpful for when we know the word, but we don't know the specific meaning of the word. Some words have more than one meaning. The word *pound* is used differently in each of the following sentences:

- We needed a pound of flour.
- He had to pound on the door to get their attention.

The two words have two different meanings. The first sentence with the word *pound* is referring to a unit of measurement. The second sentence with the word *pound* means to beat on something, like the door.

Using context clues in this way can be especially useful for words that have multiple meanings.

Analyzing Nuances of Word Meaning and Figures of Speech
Nuance means a slight difference in meaning. Students should know that one word can mean more than one thing. Also, similar meanings can be expressed by many different words. However, there are very few words that express exactly the same meaning. For this reason, it is important to be able to pick up on the nuances of word meaning.

Many words contain two levels of meaning: connotation and denotation. A word's **denotation** is its most literal meaning. It is the definition that can be found in the dictionary. A word's **connotation** includes its emotional and cultural associations.

When writing, authors rely on connotative meaning to create mood and talk about the characters. The following are two descriptions of a rainstorm:

- The rain slammed against the windowpane and the wind howled through the fireplace. A pair of hulking oaks next to the house cast eerie shadows as their branches trembled in the wind.

- The rain pattered against the windowpane and the wind whistled through the fireplace. A pair of stately oaks next to the house cast curious shadows as their branches swayed in the wind.

Description A paints a creepy picture for readers with strongly emotional words like *slammed*, connoting force and violence. *Howled* connotes pain or wildness, and *eerie* and *trembled* connote fear. Overall, the connotative language in this description serves to inspire fear and anxiety.

However, as can be seen in description B, swapping out a few key words completely changes the feeling of the passage. *Slammed* is replaced with the more cheerful *pattered*, and *hulking* has been swapped out for *stately*. Both words imply something large, but *hulking* is more intimidating, whereas *stately* is more respectable. *Curious* and *swayed* seem more playful than the language used in the earlier description. Although both descriptions represent roughly the same situation, the nuances of the emotional language used throughout the passages create a very different sense for readers. One makes you feel scared. The other makes you feel safe.

Practice Test #1

Rainy Day

1   "Please, Mom! Please!" cried Sarah. "Please, may I go in the backyard and jump on the trampoline?"

2   "No," answered her mother. "It has been raining all morning. Even though the sun has come out, the trampoline is still wet. Jumping on a wet trampoline can be very dangerous."

3   "But, Mom . . ." exclaimed Sarah.

4   "I said no, young lady. Perhaps you should go read a good book or play in your room for a while until the trampoline dries out."

5   Sarah slowly climbed the stairs to her room. She had been waiting since breakfast for the rain to stop. She really wanted to practice doing a front flip on the trampoline. She was very disappointed. Now, what would she do all day?

6   Opening the door to her room, Sarah walked over to the bookcase to look for a book to read like her mother had suggested. As she looked over each title, she felt sure she had already read all of them. None of them seemed exciting enough to read again at the moment.

7   In fact, nothing seemed exciting enough to make her feel better. The puzzle on her desk only needed a few more pieces before it was finished, but that would be boring. Her doll, Molly, needed a bath, but that would only keep her busy for a few minutes. She could use her new paints to create a nice painting for her dad's office, but she couldn't think of anything creative to draw at the moment. All she could think about were front flips.

8   As Sarah stood in the doorway looking around her room, she decided to just take a nap to pass the time. Surely, she thought, by the time I wake up, the trampoline will be dry. Then, I can practice my front flips.

9   Sarah ran to her bed, jumped high in the air, and flopped down on the bed. As the mattress springs creaked, an idea came to her. Her bed was almost as bouncy as her trampoline. She could just practice her front flips by jumping on her bed!

10   Sarah threw her pillow off the bed. She planted her feet firmly, squatted down, and leapt into the air as she pulled herself into a ball. She felt confident this front flip would be a success and she would land on her feet, ready to do it again.

11   THWACK! CRACK! Sarah knew from the pain and the tears in her eyes that something had gone terribly wrong.

12   "Mom! Mom! HELP!" Sarah screamed from her room.

1. Sarah thought about doing all except which of the following activities in her room?
    a. Painting a picture
    b. Finishing a puzzle
    c. Watching TV
    d. Reading a book

2. Based on the evidence in the story, what do you think happened to Sarah at the end?
    a. Her puzzle fell off her desk.
    b. She got hurt jumping on the bed.
    c. She remembered which book she had not read yet.
    d. She thought of something she could paint for her dad's office.

3. Which sentence from this passage tells the reader that Sarah was physically upset?
    a. "Now, what would she do all day?"
    b. "Sarah slowly climbed the stairs to her room."
    c. "All she could think about were front flips."
    d. "None of them seemed exciting enough to read again at the moment."

4. Reread paragraph 2. What can you infer might be dangerous about jumping on a wet trampoline?
    a. You can't jump very high when the trampoline mat is wet.
    b. The springs holding the mat can get rusty and break.
    c. Jumping on a wet trampoline is an easy way to catch a cold.
    d. It is easy to fall and hurt yourself on a wet trampoline mat.

5. What is the best definition of the word disappointed in paragraph 5?
    a. Bored
    b. Let down
    c. Angry
    d. Busy

6. Which of the following sentences has the correct sequence of events?
    a. Sarah thought about painting something for her dad's office before breakfast.
    b. Sarah thought about taking a nap before she finished her puzzle.
    c. Sarah jumped on her bed before she asked to jump on the trampoline.
    d. Sarah threw her pillow off the bed before she jumped on the bed.

Weather Safety

1   What do you usually do during summer break? Do you stay inside all day where it is cool, playing games, reading a book, or watching TV? Or do you prefer to do things outside, like riding your bike, going for a swim, or jumping on a trampoline? No matter which activity is your favorite, there are three very important things to remember when you go outside to play, especially when the temperature is very high.

2   First, always remember to drink a lot of water. Your body needs water to keep your organs working properly. When your body gets hot, the water in your body slowly seeps out through the pores in your skin to form sweat. Although it may stink, sweat is your body's way of cooling you so you don't overheat. So, it is important to drink plenty of water to replace the water you sweat out.

3   Second, decide if you are dressed correctly for the activity you want to do. Sports in the summer months can be dangerous, so it is important to dress appropriately for them. For example, if you are going to ride your bike in the driveway, do you have on your helmet? It only takes one wrong movement of your bicycle wheel to cause a fall, so you must protect your brain from being injured if you fall down. If you are going swimming, do you have a pair of goggles to keep the chlorine from burning your eyes? If you plan to go skateboarding, elbow and knee pads are a good choice to protect yourself if you fall.

4   Third, consider the weather for the day before you plan your activity. You can even ask Mom or Dad to help you with this. If the weather calls for rainstorms, the safest choice is to stay inside. Along with rain, storms also produce thunder and lightning. Many people think the loud roar of thunder is very scary, and lightning is very dangerous. Being struck by lightning can cause bodily injuries and requires a stay in the hospital. Understanding the weather will also give you an idea about the conditions outside. Rain not only makes things wet, but it also makes things slippery. It is easy to slip and fall on wet cement if you are not careful.

5   Unfortunately, the bad weather sometimes ruins fun plans. Reschedule your activity for another day when it will be safe to play outside. It is better to be safe than sorry.

7. Why do you think the author wrote this passage?
    a. To make readers laugh and enjoy what they are reading
    b. To remind kids that they should check the weather before breakfast
    c. To convince readers that protective body gear is not needed
    d. To explain how knowing the weather conditions can help keep you safe

8. After reading this passage, why do you think Sarah's mom didn't want her to jump on the wet trampoline in the first passage?
    a. Rain can make things slippery, and slipping on something can cause a fall.
    b. Sarah didn't drink enough water at breakfast, and she wouldn't be able to sweat.
    c. She was trying to trick Sarah into reading a book.
    d. Helmets should be worn during all outside activities.

9. In this passage, the word <u>reschedule</u> refers to which of the following?
    a. Picking another day to have fun outside
    b. Trouble deciding what you like to do outside
    c. The weather portion of a news broadcast
    d. To do something over and over again

10. Which sentence best summarizes paragraph 4?

    a. Stay inside during rainstorms because they are dangerous.

    b. It is important to decide how the weather might affect your activities.

    c. Always wear safety equipment when doing outdoor activities.

    d. Playing outside causes your body to become hot and sweaty.

11. Explain a time when you have used weather safety. Use evidence from the passage to support your answer.

One day it started thunder storming so I rescheduled my visit to the park and stayed home safely. The text says, "you should reschedule your activity for another day", this is because, "it is easy to slip and fall on wet cement".

12. What is the meaning of the last sentence in the passage? Use evidence from the passage to support your answer.

The sentence means it's better reschedule an activity

if there's bad weather than be sorry for yourself because

you had an injurey in bad weather, or had an accident

because you are not wearing proper equipment.

Real-Life Hero

1   As he stood at the bottom of the ladder, Kase watched as all of his friends ran around in the giant treehouse. It was a treehouse like he had never seen before. There were giant windows covered with swinging shutters. A bridge led to rock walls and swings and slides that twisted in all directions. Everything about the treehouse seemed to sparkle.

2   Kase really wanted to go up and join in the fun. But he was scared. He didn't like tall things that were high off the ground. They made him sweat, and his stomach squeezed into knots the size of baseballs. Sometimes he wondered why he was such a baby.

3   "Meow, meow."

4   Kase slowly looked around. Did he just hear a cat? "Meow, meow."

5   Kase began to walk around looking for a cat. He didn't see one, but he could still hear the cries.

6   "Meow, meow."

7   Out of the corner of his eye, Kase saw something move. "Meow, meow." The sound was getting louder. "Meow, meow." Then, he saw it. A tiny white kitten peeked its head around the edge of the slide. It appeared to be stuck under the slide. "Meow, meow."

8   Carefully, Kase wiggled the kitten out of the tight spot. He looked the kitten over, checking for an injury. The kitten seemed unharmed as it snuggled up in Kase's arms.

9   Kase called out to his friends as he held the kitten up like a trophy, showing them what he had found. His friends came rushing out of the treehouse, climbing down to inspect the kitten.

10   As his friends stood around him petting the kitten, Kase smiled to himself. He had been so busy looking for the kitten that he had forgotten all about the treehouse. Now, instead of feeling sad because he couldn't climb up to play with his friends, he was proud he had just rescued the kitten. Maybe he wasn't such a baby after all. Maybe he was a real-life hero who just happened to like his feet on the ground!

13. Which of the following statements is an opinion?
    a. "A tiny white kitten peeked its head around the edge of the slide." X
    b. "As he stood at the bottom of the ladder, Kase watched as all of his friends ran around in the giant treehouse." X
    c. "He didn't like tall things that were high off the ground."
    d. "Everything about the treehouse seemed to sparkle." X

14. Why did Kase forget about climbing up to the treehouse? _He had been so busy looking for the kitten._

15. Since Kase doesn't like to climb off the ground, readers can assume which of the following?
    a. He knew he needed to rescue a kitten.
    b. He thinks real superheroes must fly.
    c. He is afraid of heights.
    d. He doesn't want to play with his friends.

59

16. Explain what you think would have happened to the kitten if Kase hadn't found it. Use evidence from the passage to support your answer.

> I think the kitten would grown hungry and thirsty because
>
> it was stuck under a slide.

17. All except which of the following words can be used to replace the word sparkle in paragraph 1?
    a. Glimmer
    b. Gleam
    c. Twinkle
    d. Dim

18. Which of the following could be the setting of the story?
    a. A mountaintop during winter
    b. Someone's backyard on a nice spring day
    c. A corner of the cafeteria
    d. An indoor waterpark

A Surprise for Marybeth

1   Every day when Ellie and Marybeth walked home from school, they passed Mr. Jack's ice cream stand. Kids were always crowded around Mr. Jack, shouting out which kind of ice cream they wanted to buy. There were so many flavors—Strawberry Sunshine, Perfectly Peppermint, Crispy Coconut, and Double Delight Chocolate Chunk. The girls always waved hello to Mr. Jack, but they never stopped.

2   Sometimes Marybeth and Ellie talked about what flavor they would get at Mr. Jack's. Ellie wanted a Double Delight Chocolate Chunk ice cream cone so bad she could almost taste it. Marybeth was dying to try the Perfectly Peppermint. And they agreed: They would order the big ice cream cone that held three giant scoops of ice cream.

3   But it was all just wishful thinking. Ellie and Marybeth never got to stop at Mr. Jack's because their mom worked two jobs. She didn't like either of the jobs, but she said she had to pay the bills. There was never any extra money for ice cream cones. Eventually, Marybeth stopped asking, but Ellie was little and didn't really understand. She asked Mom about the ice cream every day.

4   Marybeth knew she was never going to get ice cream from Mr. Jack's, just like she knew she wasn't getting a present for her birthday. It was tomorrow.

5   At school the next day, Mrs. Crenshaw made her wear a silly birthday hat all day. Davy, in her math class, tried to give her a pet frog, but Mr. Jenkins freaked out when he realized there was an animal in his classroom. He threw Davy's frog right out the window!

6   As they walked home, Marybeth and Ellie laughed about Mr. Jenkins and the frog as they noticed Mr. Jack waiving them over to his ice cream stand. They wondered why he wanted to speak with them.

7   The girls couldn't believe their ears when Mr. Jack told them they could pick any ice cream cone they wanted. He said today they both deserved his biggest ice cream cone.

8   Marybeth and Ellie were so excited. They thanked and hugged Mr. Jack two times each.

9   Oh, the ice cream was so cold and refreshing. It was just as delicious as Marybeth and Ellie had imagined. Mr. Jack might never know it, but he had given Marybeth the best birthday present ever!

19. What kind of ice cream cone did Marybeth probably enjoy for her birthday?
    a. Strawberry Sunshine
    b. Perfectly Peppermint
    c. Crispy Coconut
    d. Double Delight Chocolate Chunk

20. Which of the following was a result of Ellie's mom having to pay bills?
    a. Marybeth and Ellie could not buy ice cream cones.
    b. Mr. Jack gave Ellie an ice cream cone for her birthday.
    c. Ellie's mom had to work three jobs.
    d. Marybeth got a nice birthday present.

21. What is the conflict in the story?
    a. Mr. Jack didn't have enough ice cream for all of the kids.
    b. Mr. Jenkins wouldn't let Marybeth keep the frog.
    c. Ellie's mom had to work two jobs.
    d. The girls didn't have money for ice cream cones.

22. How did Mr. Jack know Marybeth and Ellie couldn't afford to buy ice cream? Use evidence from the passage to support your answer.

Mr. Jack knew because Ellie and Marybeth always walked by his ice-cream stand and waved to him, but never stopped to get Mr. Jack's ice-cream.

23. Which word best describes Marybeth?
    a. Understanding
    b. Spiteful
    c. Demanding
    d. Unfriendly

24. Which of the following details in the story is incorrect?
    a. Ellie is the youngest of the two sisters.
    b. Mr. Jack gave an ice cream cone to Marybeth and Ellie.
    c. Marybeth had to wear a silly birthday hat at school.
    d. The girls' mother likes both of her jobs very much.

Fix-It Freddie's

1 School was out for summer, and all of Freddie's friends had exciting plans. Some of them were going on vacation. Others were going to spend their summer riding their bikes and playing at the pool. All of that did sound like fun, but Freddie had other things in mind.

2 Freddie wanted a new skateboard. It was all he could think about these days. He'd asked his brother, Will, to lend him the money, but Will didn't have a job. The little bit of money he did manage to come up with he used to buy parts for the old car he was fixing up.

3 Freddie's mom and dad said he needed to get a job if he wanted money to buy a skateboard. But getting a job was impossible. Freddie had visited several dozen businesses in town. Not one of them would hire a twelve-year-old.

4 But Freddie came up with a plan, and he was sure it would work. He was going to start his own business and earn enough money to buy a skateboard and whatever else he wanted.

5 Freddie spent an entire afternoon designing a business flyer. The name of his business was going to be Fix-It Freddie's. He listed jobs he knew how to do. He could trim trees, mow yards, clean out gutters, mend fences, paint houses, and wash cars. Freddie was also willing to do special request jobs that weren't on his flyer. He finalized the flyer by adding his phone number so customers could call him.

6 It only took one afternoon for Freddie to leave a flyer in every mailbox in his neighborhood. All he had to do now was wait for the phone to ring. He couldn't wait to get his first customer, but he was a little worried at the same time. What if no one called?

7 That evening, Freddie's first customer called. It was Mrs. Jenkins, and she needed a tree trimmed in her backyard. Mr. Wilson called because he wanted his car washed. Old Man Potter around the corner wanted his yard mowed every week until school started. And that was just the beginning. The phone kept ringing and ringing. Everyone in the neighborhood needed jobs done, and Freddie's schedule was getting full.

8 In fact, Freddie was getting so many calls, he didn't know how he was going to keep up with all the jobs. He never dreamed his business would get off to such a great start. Will agreed to come work with him as long as he and Freddie split the money they made equally.

9 They were going to be rich! Well, maybe not rich, but Freddie would definitely make enough money to buy a new skateboard, and Will just might be able to buy the rest of the parts he needed to get his car running.

25. Who was the third person to call Freddie to schedule a job?
  a. Will
  b. Old Man Potter
  c. Mr. Wilson
  d. Mrs. Jenkins

26. True or False. Freddie put a flyer on every door in his neighborhood. _____ *False* _____

27. If you opened your own business, what would you name it? What type of service would you provide? Write in complete sentences.

> I would name my business, Doggie Daycare, because it's catchy and I love helping dogs.

28. What is something we can infer about Freddie's character?
    a. He gets along well with his friends at school.
    b. He is a hard worker.
    c. He likes to buy expensive things.
    d. He looks up to his brother.

29. What is a synonym for *designing*?
    a. Copying
    b. Creating
    c. Duplicating
    d. Imitating

30. Which of the following statements about this passage is correct?
    a. Some of Freddie's friends were going to school this summer.
    b. Freddie's grandma told him to get a job to earn money for his skateboard.
    c. Freddie had so much business, he asked his brother to work with him.
    d. There were several businesses in town that would hire twelve-year-olds.

Fix It Freddie's

We do odd jobs!

* Tree Trimming

* Gutter Cleaning

* Car Washing

* Yard Mowing

*Fence Mending

* House Painting

No job is too big or too small!

Call Freddie:

292-345-0899

31. What would be the best tool for Freddie to use to organize his busy schedule?
    a. Notebook
    b. Chalkboard
    c. Thumbtacks
    d. Calendar

32. Which of the following is a statement Freddie could add to his flyer?
    a. Customers will need to provide lunch.
    b. We do special request jobs.
    c. We take breaks from 11:00 a.m. to 12 p.m.
    d. We don't have our own tools.

33. Why did Freddie pass out a flyer for his business? _So that people can call him because his phone number was on the flyer._

34. If Freddie wanted to alphabetize the jobs listed on his flyer, which of the following would be correct?
    a. Car Washing, Yard Mowing, Fence Mending
    b. Tree Trimming, Gutter Cleaning, Car Washing
    c. Car Washing, Fence Mending, House Painting
    d. Gutter Cleaning, Yard Mowing, Fence Mending

35. What error did Freddie make on his flyer?
    a. The word *trimming* is spelled wrong.
    b. The phone number is incorrect.
    c. There is no hyphen between the words *Fix* and *It*.
    d. There is no picture of Freddie on the flyer.

36. All except which of the following would be great ways for Freddie to advertise his business?
    a. Wearing a T-shirt with his company name on the back
    b. Putting signs in customers' yards once he has completed the jobs
    c. Asking his customers to refer his company to someone they know
    d. Putting bumper stickers with his company logo on all of his customers' cars without asking

66

Terrified Tom

1   "ACK!" screamed Tom.

2   "What's wrong?" replied Suzie as she ran across the playground toward Tom.

3   "There is a bug on my arm!" Tom stood frozen under the tree. He was as still as a statue you would see in a museum.

4   "Bug? What kind of bug?" Suzie said as she looked closely at the funny-looking bug on Tom's arm.

5   "Don't touch it! If you make it mad, it might bite me." Tom looked scared.

6   Suzie didn't know what kind of bug it was either, but it was kind of cute. The round little bug crawled a few inches up Tom's arm. He looked terrified.

7   "It's red and black," said Tom. "Don't the colors red and black mean an animal is poisonous? If it bites me, I'm going to die!" He was starting to panic.

8   Suzie rolled her eyes at Tom. "Don't be silly, Tom. You're thinking of snakes. Red and yellow snakes are poisonous. I don't think this bug is big enough to hurt you." She could tell Tom wasn't convinced because he was turning a little pale.

9   "I think you're wrong. I'm pretty sure the color red on its back means it's poisonous!" Tom said in a panic. Sweat was starting to form on his forehead.

10   She was beginning to get worried. Maybe Tom was right. "You're right! I think the spots are a bad sign," replied Suzie. Maybe this bug was poisonous. "My cousin, Rob, got bitten by a spider once. It had spots on its back. His leg swelled up as big as a volleyball. My Aunt Becky had to take him to the hospital. The doctor had to use a needle to pop his leg like a balloon before it exploded."

11   Tom started to cry. He hated bugs. He hated hospitals. He hated doctors. And he hated needles. This wasn't going to turn out well for him.

12   "Don't cry, Tom. I'll go get Mrs. Henderson and tell her to call 9-1-1. They will send someone to get this bug. And they will send an ambulance in case it bites you." Suzie only hoped that help could get there in time. The red and black bug with dangerous spots was starting to inch its way farther up Tom's arm now.

13   Suzie ran as fast as she could across the playground to get Mrs. Henderson. As they both hurried back over to Tom, Suzie told Mrs. Henderson all about the dangerous bug that was about to bite him.

14   "Don't get too close, Mrs. Henderson!" cried Tom. "If you make it mad, it might bite me!"

15   "Why, Tom! Don't be afraid. I don't see any hospitals in your future," Mrs. Henderson said as she scooped up the little bug in the palm of her hand and held it close for Tom and Suzie to see. "This harmless little cutie is a ladybug!"

37. Out of the following events in the story, which one happened second?
    a. Suzie went to get Mrs. Henderson for help.
    b. Mrs. Henderson removed the bug from Tom's arm.
    c. Suzie tells Tom that Rob had to go to the hospital.
    d. Tom stood as still as a statue.

38. In paragraph 15, the word harmless means _it can't harm or hurt you._

_____.

39. Which of the following statements makes a comparison?
    a. "I don't think this bug is big enough to hurt you."
    b. "His leg swelled up as big as a volleyball."
    c. "Suzie rolled her eyes at Tom."
    d. "They will send someone to get this bug."

40. Which statement creates a visual image for the reader?
    a. "She was beginning to get worried."
    b. "Sweat was starting to form on his forehead."
    c. "Maybe this bug was poisonous."
    d. "I don't see any hospitals in your future."

68

41. Explain how Suzie's decision to go get Mrs. Henderson for help was a good one. Use evidence from the passage to support your answer.

It was a good decision because the kids would've

never kown it was a harmless ladybug and

Tom probaly would stand still for a while until

the bug flew away.

42. All except which of the following are exaggerations?
    a. "If it bites me, I'm going to die."
    b. "The doctor had to use a needle to pop his leg like a balloon before it exploded."
    c. "His leg swelled up as big as a volleyball."
    d. "I don't think this bug is big enough to hurt you."

Emergency 9-1-1

1   The National Emergency Number Association provides an emergency calling system for individuals in need of immediate help. This service is available to everyone within the United States. However, it is only available in some international countries.

HOW TO CALL
2   Using a landline or cellular phone, dial the numbers 9-1-1. The call is free.

WHO CAN CALL
3   Anyone in an emergency situation or requiring immediate assistance can call 9-1-1.

WHEN TO CALL
4   If someone is in a situation in which they feel unsafe or have a medical emergency, they should call 9-1-1. A few examples of emergencies are a fire, a sudden medical problem (trouble breathing, serious injury), or a car accident (witnessed or involved).

PLACED CALLS
5   When a caller dials 9-1-1, an operator will answer and confirm that there is an emergency situation. The operator will then ask the caller to describe the problem. The caller will also be asked to provide an address or general location of the emergency.

6   While the caller is providing this information, the operator will work to dispatch emergency responders to the caller's location. Depending on the kind of emergency, firefighters, police, ambulances, or all three will be sent to the emergency location.

7   The operator will stay on the line with the caller until help arrives. The operator's job is to keep the caller calm and give directions regarding how to handle the emergency until help arrives.

ACCIDENTAL CALLS
8   If a caller makes an accidental call to 9-1-1, the caller should stay on the line to let the operator know the call was placed by mistake.

PRANK CALLS
9   No one should ever make prank calls to 9-1-1. Someone with a real emergency could need help. If a caller has an operator's line tied up as a joke, someone might not be getting the help they really need.

43. What number can you call if there is an emergency and you need immediate help? _9-1-1_____

44. What are the underlined words throughut the text called?
    a. Headlines
    b. Titles
    c. Headings
    d. Questions

45. Why is it important not to make prank calls to 9-1-1? _Because someone_
with a real emergency could need help

46. What does the word <u>dispatch</u> mean?
   a. To email
   b. To migrate
   c. To send out
   d. To pull back

47. According to paragraph 4, what should you do if you witness or are involved in a car accident? Use evidence from the passage to support your answer.

I would call 9-1-1 because I would be in a

emergency situation.

48. Why does the author have the information in this passage broken into sections?
   a. To take up space on the page
   b. To confuse readers with a lot of information
   c. To make the passage look nice for the reader
   d. To organize a lot of information for the reader

Mimi's Pail, Part 1

1   Dayton and Jacob had thought it was a good idea at the time. They always fished down at the lake. Every summer they stayed at the farm with Jacob's grandparents. Dayton's mom didn't have summers off and had to work in the city. It was more fun to stay at the farm with Jacob than to stay home by himself and do chores.

2   Dayton and Jacob spent most days down at the lake. Mimi packed a pail for them to take fishing every day. It was Mimi's favorite pail, one that her mother had given her when she was a little girl. It was always full of ham sandwiches and apples and two large mason jars filled with ice-cold sweet tea.

3   The fishing had been good all morning. They had already caught two trout and four catfish. They rigged their lines up again and then sat down to eat lunch. Fishing sure does make you hungry. As they ate, they talked about how Mimi was going to be excited to fry up some fresh fish for dinner that night. Maybe she would make mashed potatoes too.

4   They ate everything Mimi had packed in the pail and wished today had been the day she'd surprised them with some chocolate cookies for dessert. But since there were no cookies in the bottom of the pail, a quick game of Kick the Can would have to do.

5   They kicked the pail very gently so it wouldn't get damaged. The pail wobbled and rolled and bounced along the ground with each gentle kick. Dayton and Jacob giggled as they took turns kicking. The game was such fun. It was fun, at least, until things went wrong.

6   It was Jacob's turn to kick the can. As he swung his leg forward to kick, his foot got caught on a tree root. Instead of kicking, Jacob flew up in the air and crashed right down on Mimi's pail.

7   Dayton helped Jacob up, and they looked down to find that Mimi's pail had been smashed as flat as a pancake. They stared at each other in disbelief. They'd never meant to damage the pail. How were they ever going to explain this to Mimi? She was going to ground them for the rest of the summer for sure.

49. Why was Mimi's pail so special? _____

50. What is the conflict in this passage?
    a. There were no chocolate cookies in the pail.
    b. Dayton had to stay home by himself and do chores.
    c. The boys smashed Mimi's special pail.
    d. They had only caught two trout and four catfish.

51. Explain how Mimi's pail was smashed. Use evidence from the passage to support your answer.

```
┌─────────────────────────────────────────────────────────────┐
│                                                             │
│   _____   │
│                                                             │
│                                                             │
│   _____   │
│                                                             │
│                                                             │
│   _____   │
│                                                             │
│                                                             │
└─────────────────────────────────────────────────────────────┘
```

52. Which of the following statements is a simile?
    a. "The fishing had been good all morning."
    b. "It was fun, at least, until things went wrong."
    c. "Dayton helped Jacob up, and they looked down to find that Mimi's pail had been smashed as flat as a pancake."
    d. "It was Mimi's favorite pail, one that her mother had given her when she was a little girl."

53. What is the setting of this story?
    a. Countryside
    b. Great Depression
    c. Urban city
    d. Wild West

54. What are some details in the passage that let the reader know that it does NOT take place in modern times?

_____

_____

_____

_____

_____

Mimi's Pail, Part 2

1   They stayed at the lake until it was almost dark. They'd given up on catching any more fish. Without Mimi's pail, they couldn't carry them all home anyway. Letting them go back into the lake was hard. After all, they had eaten lunch a long time ago, and now they were starving.

2   Jacob and Dayton knew if they didn't get home before dark, Mimi would start to worry that something bad had happened to them. She'd call the sheriff and demand a search party be sent out to look for them. The whole town would swarm the lake with flashlights and hound dogs. And all of that would be for nothing. They weren't lost or injured. They were just scared.

3   As they walked home up the hill, they tried to come up with a good story to tell Mimi. Jacob said a bear was big enough to smash a pail, but Dayton reminded him that there weren't any bears in the area. Dayton suggested that a bobcat could have smashed the pail, but Jacob said a bobcat would have eaten them and left the pail alone.

4   The boys were too busy talking to realize how far they had walked. They looked up to see they were standing in the yard. The porch light came on, and Mimi stepped out the front door. She was wiping her hands on her apron, and she looked really mad.

5   "Boys," she said, "what took you so long to get home? I was about to send Sheriff Colter out to look for you."

6   The boys just stood there, speechless.

7   "Well, come on in and wash up for supper. Since you were gone so long, I figured you probably didn't have much luck catching today. Maybe tomorrow will be better, and I can fry up some fish then. Say, where's your lunch pail?"

8   They both walked toward the porch.

9   "What's wrong with you two?" Mimi asked.

10   "We accidentally crushed your special pail, Mimi," Jacob said as tears streamed down his face.

11   "We were just playing a little game of Kick the Can until Jacob fell," Dayton added nervously. "It really was an accident. We're really sorry about your special pail, Mimi."

12   The sound of Mimi's laughter eased their worry a little, but they weren't exactly sure what she thought was so funny. It was her favorite pail, after all.

13   "Why, that old thing? That's just a pretty little pail I bought years ago down at the Mercantile. Mr. Wickshaw sold it to me for ten cents!" Mimi chuckled. "I just told you it was special because I didn't want you going down to the lake and losing it. I didn't want to keep going back to the Mercantile every time you boys lost a bucket or left it down at the lake. But I guess we can walk over tomorrow and get a new one." She laughed so hard her belly was shaking. "Maybe we should get a couple of extras just in case!"

55. If Mimi had called Sheriff Colter, why would he have sent hound dogs to the lake to look for the boys?

_____

_____

56. Why wasn't Mimi angry about her special pail being smashed?
    a. It was really just an ordinary pail she bought at the Mercantile.
    b. She didn't really like her mother very much.
    c. She would let Jacob and Dayton get away with anything.
    d. She wanted to buy them new lunch boxes for Christmas.

57. What type of writing is this?
    a. Narrative
    b. Informative
    c. Speech
    d. Persuasive

58. Was Mimi really angry with the boys when she stepped out on the front porch? Use evidence from the passage to support your answer.

_____

_____

_____

_____

_____

59. What is a synonym for the word <u>swarm</u>?
    a. Crowd
    b. Retreat
    c. Small
    d. Tree

60. How much did Mimi's pail cost? _____

Answer Explanations #1

1. C: Paragraph 7 discusses all of the activities Sarah has going on in her room. Watching TV is not mentioned in the paragraph.

2. B: Look for clues in the story. Words such as *THWACK! CRACK!* hint that Sarah might have hit part of her body on the foot of the bed, or she might have fallen off the bed. *Pain* and *tears* are words that tell readers Sarah's body has been physically hurt. When children hurt themselves, they usually cry out for a parent to come help them.

3. B: Your body language can express that you are physically upset. Think about when you get upset. Do you hang your head down? Do you plop down in the chair? Do you sigh or throw your hands in the air? Choice *B* tells readers about Sarah's body language as she climbed the stairs. If she had been excited to go to her room, she might have run up the stairs.

4. D: What does *infer* mean? Take what you know from the story and add it to what you already know to make an inference. For example, have you ever stepped on a surface that was wet? If so, then you know it's slippery. You might have even fallen down. You also know that Sarah's trampoline was wet. Combine those two ideas. If you know wet surfaces like Sarah's trampoline can be slippery, then it is correct to think that she could easily slip and fall down.

5. B: Use the clues in paragraph 5 to decide what the word <u>disappointed</u> means. The important clues are how Sarah climbed the stairs, how long she had been patiently waiting, and that jumping on the trampoline was what she really wanted to be doing instead of going to her room. The phrase *let down* is the best choice here.

6. D: This is the only answer choice that lists the events in the correct order.

7. D: The passage is written to tell readers about weather safety. The passage is not funny, and it does not try to convince the reader to avoid protective body gear or check the weather before breakfast.

8. A: The author states that rain makes things slippery and can cause a fall. If Sarah's trampoline was wet, then it is very possible that she could easily fall down and get hurt while jumping.

9. A: The prefix *re-* means "to do something again." When you schedule something, you pick a day or a time to do it.

10. B: Summarizing a paragraph means deciding how to put everything the author is telling you into one sentence. This means the sentence must tell what the whole paragraph talks about instead of giving specific details.

11. SUGGESTED: *Last week, I went to my friend Mary's house. She has a pool, and we really wanted to go swimming. It was not very sunny outside, and the sky was a little dark. We didn't know if it was going to rain, but we did know that rain sometimes brings thunder and lightning. Lightning is very bad when you are in the pool. We decided to wait a little bit to see if it was going to rain.*

12. SUGGESTED: *The author says "It is better to be safe than sorry" because rescheduling an activity due to the rain or wearing a helmet for a summer sport is much better than the bad consequences that can follow. It is always better to be extra careful and to think ahead so nobody gets hurt!*

13. D: An opinion is what someone thinks about something. Kase thinks the treehouse sparkles. The rest of his friends might just think it is an ordinary treehouse.

14. SUGGESTED: *Kase forgot about being scared to climb up to the treehouse because he got distracted trying to rescue the kitten.*

15. C: The word *heights* refers to something that is high off the ground (rollercoasters, treehouses, rooftops). Kase has a strong reaction when he thinks about his feet leaving the ground. So, he is afraid of heights.

16. SUGGESTED: *If Kase hadn't found the kitten, it probably would have kept crying for help. It would have gotten thirsty and hungry. It would have been scared because it was all alone. The kitten might have been stuck under the slide until another group of kids came to play.*

17. D: The word *dim* means "dark" or "not very much light." This is the opposite meaning of <u>sparkle</u>.

18. B: The setting is most likely someone's backyard on a nice spring day. This is because large treehouses are usually in someone's backyard, and not on a mountaintop, in a cafeteria, or an indoor water park.

19. B: Paragraph 1 tells the reader that Marybeth dreams of trying Perfectly Peppermint ice cream.

20. A: Marybeth and Ellie could not buy ice cream cones because there was no money left over after their mom paid the bills.

21. D: The conflict in the story is the problem the main character (or characters) faces. In this story, the problem is that Marybeth and Ellie really want an ice cream cone, but they don't have any money.

22. SUGGESTED: *Many of the kids buy ice cream from Mr. Jack every day after school. Over the school year, he has noticed that Marybeth and Ellie are the only two kids that don't stop by his stand. Almost all kids like ice cream, so he had to know that there was something keeping them from getting ice cream.*

23. A: Marybeth can be described as understanding because she realizes that her mother is working very hard to pay the bills. She understands that it is more important to pay the bills than it is to buy treats like ice cream.

24. D: In the passage, we know that Ellie is the youngest of the two sisters, that Mr. Jack gave an ice cream cone to Marybeth and Ellie, and that Marybeth had to wear a silly birthday hat at school. We are not told that the girls' mother likes her jobs.

25. B: Paragraph 7 tells readers that Old Man Potter was the third person to call Freddie to schedule a job.

26. False: Freddie put a flyer in every mailbox in his neighborhood.

27. SUGGESTED: *If I opened my own business, I would call it Sew Something. Since I am good at sewing, I would offer to sew or mend things for customers.*

28. B: Freddie was determined to earn enough money for his skateboard. Doing manual labor is difficult. Readers can infer that he is a hard worker because he is determined to make his business successful so he can buy a new skateboard.

29. B: A synonym is a word that means the same as another word. *Creating* means the same as *designing*.

30. C: Paragraph 8 tells readers that Freddie had so much business, he had to ask his brother to work with him.

31. D: Using a calendar is the best way for Freddie to keep track of the jobs he has each day and what time they start.

32. B: If Freddie is willing to do jobs other than those listed on his flyer, he should let people know they can request a special job be done.

33. SUGGESTED: *Freddie passed out flyers for his business because they are inexpensive to make, and it was easy for him to walk around the neighborhood to pass them out. This was a good way to advertise his business and provide people with his phone number.*

34. C: Choice *C* is the only list that is alphabetized correctly.

35. C: The passage states that the name of the business will be Fix-It Freddie's. When Freddie made his flyer, he left out the hyphen between the words *Fix* and *It*.

36. D: Business owners should never do anything to a customer's property without asking.

37. C: In paragraph 10, Suzie tells Tom about her cousin, Rob, getting bitten by a spider and having to go to the hospital. The events in order in the story are D, C, A, B.

38. ANSWER: *The word* harmless *means "not harmful" or "that something will not hurt."*

39. B: Choice *B* compares the size of Rob's leg to the size of a volleyball, so this is the correct answer.

40. B: Choice *B* helps create a visual picture for readers—we can imagine the sweat on Tom's forehead.

41. SUGGESTED: *Since Suzie and Tom couldn't decide if the bug was poisonous or not, it was a good decision to ask an adult. No one should ever call 9-1-1 unless they are absolutely sure there is an emergency.*

42. D: Exaggeration means "to make a statement that isn't necessarily accurate in order to make a point." This is often done when telling a story. Choice *D* does not make an exaggeration.

43. ANSWER: *Dial 9-1-1 if there is an emergency.*

44. C: Headings are used to divide a text into smaller parts.

45. ANSWER: *No one should make prank calls to 9-1-1 because it ties up the phone line. This means that someone who really needs help might not be able to get through to an operator.*

46. C: The word dispatch means "to send out." The 9-1-1 operator *sends out*, or dispatches, help to the location of the caller in emergency cases.

47. SUGGESTED: *You should call 9-1-1 if you witness a car accident or if you are involved in a car accident.*

48. D: Dividing large informational texts into smaller sections helps organize the information for the reader. The smaller sections make the information easier to read.

49. ANSWER: *Paragraph 2 tells readers that Mimi's mother gave her the pail when she was a little girl.*

50. C: The conflict, or problem, in the story is that the boys accidentally smashed Mimi's special pail.

51. ANSWER: *Mimi's pail was smashed on accident. Jacob was trying to kick the can when he tripped on a tree root. When he fell down, he landed on Mimi's pail and flattened it.*

52. C: A simile is a comparison of two things using the words *like* or *as*. Choice *C* compares the thickness of the smashed pail to the thickness of a pancake.

53. A: Readers can assume the story takes place in the countryside because Jacob's grandparents live on a farm.

54. SUGGESTED: *The reader might infer the story does not take place in modern times because the boys use a pail as a lunch box. Most kids now use a cloth or plastic lunch box. Also, the boys' drinks are packed in mason jars. Today, kids use thermos bottles.*

55. SUGGESTED: *Hound dogs are very good at picking up scents. They would have been able to pick up the boys' scent and hunt until they found them.*

56. A: In paragraph 14, Mimi reveals that the pail really had no special value to her.

57. A: This type of writing is a narrative. Narratives tell stories.

58. SUGGESTED: *Mimi was not angry at the boys for smashing her pail. When she came outside, she didn't actually know they had damaged it. However, she was beginning to get worried that something bad had happened to them because they were so late getting home.*

59. A: The search party would swarm, or crowd, the lake to look for the boys.

60. ANSWER: *Mimi's pail cost ten cents.*

Practice Test #2

Walter's Vacation, Part 1

1   Walter wants to go on vacation this summer. There are so many exciting places to go, but he can't decide where he should ask his mom to take him. He decided to do some research to show his mom. If he could narrow down some of the choices, perhaps it would be easier to decide where to go.

2   Using his computer, Walter researched different kinds of vacations. He was definitely surprised to learn that there were so many types of places to visit. He could choose a water park adventure, outdoor hiking, a historical tour, famous monuments, or beach resort, just to name a few.

3   With so much information to look at, Walter felt very overwhelmed by his research. At school, Walter's teacher encouraged students to make charts to sort out information. So, he decided to create a chart to help figure out his vacation options.

Type of Vacation	Destination	Distance from Home	Method of Travel	Where to Stay	Cost
Outdoor/ Hiking/ Camping	Yellowstone National Park	1406 miles	Airplane	Tent/ RV	$2239
Water Park	Great Wolf Lodge	453 miles	Car	Lodge	$876
Amusement Park	Disney World	3274 miles	Airplane	Hotel	$5400
Historic Tour	Washington, DC	2341 miles	Airplane	Hotel	$3750

1. If Walter wanted to put the **Type of Vacation** column in alphabetical order, which one of the following would be correct?
    a. Historic Tour, Outdoor/Hiking/Camping, Water Park, Amusement Park
    b. Amusement Park, Historic Tour, Outdoor/Hiking/Camping, Water Park
    c. Water Park, Historic Tour, Outdoor/Hiking/Camping, Amusement Park
    d. Amusement Park, Outdoor/Hiking/Camping, Water Park, Historic Tour

2. Why is Walter doing research on different vacations? _____

_____

3. Which method of travel is least expensive? _____

4. What does the word **Destination** mean?
    a. City or entertainment park
    b. Place traveling to
    c. Historic landmark
    d. Vacation

5. Review the chart in the passage. Which vacation do you think Walter's mother will choose, and why? Use evidence from the passage to support your answer.

_____

_____

_____

6. Walter used his computer to do his research. All except which one of the following are other ways Walter could have researched vacations?

    a. Read a travel magazine.

    b. Check out a book about vacations from the library.

    c. Look for information in a newspaper.

    d. Ask a friend or neighbor for vacation suggestions.

Walter's Vacation, Part 2

1   A giant bucket hung high above all of the activities going on inside the lodge. Over the course of half an hour, it slowly filled with water. Just when you least expected, it spilled over, <u>soaking</u> everyone in its path. Walter stood underneath it for a long time trying to figure out exactly when it would spill next. But he grew impatient and moved on.

2   They took a spin around the lazy river. Buckets of water poured down on them at random, and the tiny <u>rapids</u> moved their inner tubes along. Walter's mom said it felt good to be lazy even if it was in a river. But Walter didn't feel so lazy because he kept falling out of his inner tube.

3   The waterslide seemed to go on forever. It twisted and turned and sloshed him all around. The water felt cool as it splish-splashed on his face and whooshed over his body. Walter giggled as he listened to his mom's squeals as she came down the slide behind him.

4   Waves crashed toward them as he <u>bobbled</u> in the wave pool. A group of kids throwing around a beach ball asked Walter to play with them. Mom watched from a lounge chair and cheered them on. Walter was really enjoying himself, and Mom seemed to be having fun too.

5   When the water park closed, Walter and Mom put on their pajamas and <u>gathered</u> in the lobby in front of the big clock tower. The animated show lasted 30 minutes. It was about how to treat the forest animals kindly and was very informative.

6   Ollie, the wolf, read everyone a bedtime story. Walter was glad he and Mom had sat close enough to see all of the pictures in Ollie's book. Mom even took a picture of Walter with Ollie when story time was over.

7   Man! Walter sure was tired after such an exciting day. As Mom tucked him into bed, he hugged her tight. "I love you, Mom. This has been the best vacation ever!"

8   Walter closed his eyes. As he drifted off to sleep, he thought about all the fun they would have again tomorrow.

7. Where did Walter and his mom choose to go on vacation?
    a. Yellowstone National Park
    b. Great Wolf Lodge
    c. Disney World
    d. Washington, DC

8. Which of the following is something the reader can infer about Walter?
    a. He knows how to swim.
    b. He is seven years old.
    c. He doesn't like to get his face wet.
    d. He snores when he sleeps.

9. Explain why Walter and his mother would wear pajamas at a water park. Use evidence from the passage to support your answer.

_____

_____

_____

_____

10. Where were Walter and his mom when the buckets randomly dumped water on them?
    a. Lazy river
    b. Wave pool
    c. Giant dumping bucket
    d. Waterslide

11. What are three words Walter uses to describe the waterslide? _____

_____

12. Which paragraph contains the underlined word that means "to go up and down"?
    a. Paragraph 1
    b. Paragraph 2
    c. Paragraph 4
    d. Paragraph 5

Preparing for a Puppy

1   Puppies are fluffy and cute. Their small size makes them easy to cuddle. Everyone wants a puppy of their own until it's time to put in the work. Yes, that's right. There are things you must do and buy in order to get ready to bring a new puppy into your home.

2   It is important to inspect your yard to make sure it is puppy friendly. Check the fence around the yard. Look for any holes where the puppy might be able to get out. Decide what area of the yard you want to train your puppy to go to the bathroom. Make sure there is a shady area where your puppy can rest on sunny days. Also, you should have a large bowl outside that your dog can use for drinking water.

3   Before your puppy comes home, you will need to get a few supplies. You will need a collar and a leash so you can take your dog for a walk each day. Inside food and water bowls will also be needed. It is best to wait to purchase puppy food until you know what kind of food your puppy needs to eat. Your new puppy will also need a nice bed to lie on, especially if you don't want it to lie on the couch. Puppies like to chew on things when they are teething, so it is a good idea to have a few toys for them. Playing with their toys will distract them from chewing on the legs of the furniture. If you plan to groom your puppy at home, you will need puppy shampoo, a brush for dog hair, and a flea collar.

4   Once you have secured your yard and bought the proper supplies, you are ready to bring your new puppy home. Your puppy will be happy, and so will you.

13. This passage is mainly about which of the following?
    a. What kind of food you need to buy for your puppy
    b. How to prepare your yard for a puppy
    c. Things you need to think about before you get a puppy
    d. Everyone loving cute puppies

14. Why do puppies need toys? Use evidence from the passage to support your answer.

_____

_____

_____

15. Which word is the opposite of the word <u>inspect</u> used in paragraph 2?
    a. Examine
    b. Study
    c. Investigate
    d. Ignore

16. The person who wrote this article is probably which of the following?
    a. Farmer
    b. Zookeeper
    c. Dog trainer
    d. Jockey

17. What three things will you need to groom your puppy at home? _____

_____

18. Is the following statement a fact or an opinion?

    "Puppies are fluffy and cute."

    a. Fact
    b. Opinion

Getting a Puppy

1   Once you have prepared your home and gotten all of the necessary items, you are ready to get your puppy. There are several places you can look to find a puppy that is just right for you and your family.

2   **First**, you can look in classified ads online. In the classified ads, you will want to search under the "Pets" section. The ad will list information about the puppy. Almost all ads will tell you if the dog is male or female, its age, and the cost. Some ads will include information such as whether or not the puppy has had its first round of shots and if it has been house trained. In addition, there will be a phone number or an email provided so you can contact the person selling the puppy. Purchasing a puppy through a classified ad is often costly but usually guarantees that you get a full-breed puppy.

3   **Second**, you can check pet stores in your area. Pet stores will often host "pet adoption" days. On these days, the store allows rescue groups to bring their puppies to the store in hopes that customers will take some or all of them home. These puppies have been rescued from the streets or turned over by owners who can't take care of them. Sometimes you will find pure-breed puppies at pet store adoptions, but usually little is known about the puppies because they were rescued. Rescue pet adoptions might be a little cheaper than a puppy from the classified ads, but not by much.

4   And **finally**, you can go to a nearby animal shelter and look at the puppies they have available for adoption. Many of these dogs have also been rescued from dangerous situations. Some have been turned in by their owners for different reasons, and some were found wandering the streets. Again, usually very little information is known about the exact breed of these dogs, but you can usually take one home for pretty cheap.

5   Wherever you choose to get a puppy, feel confident that you will pick the right puppy for your family. These puppies just want a good, loving home, and you are fully prepared!

19. Who in this passage would be the best person to ask about the kind of puppy food you will need to purchase?
    a. Previous puppy owners
    b. A pet adoption specialist
    c. The person who found the puppy
    d. Any customer in the pet store.

20. According to the passage, where would you look for a puppy if you wanted to be sure you were buying a full-breed puppy?

_____

21. What are the bolded words in the passage?
    a. Numbers
    b. Beginners
    c. Transitions
    d. Paragraphs

22. Where can you get a puppy for the least amount of money?

_____

23. The word <u>house trained</u> means which of the following?
   a. The puppy has already been taught not to go to the bathroom in the house.
   b. The puppy has been trained to look sad so it will get picked for a new home.
   c. The puppy is assigned an adoption specialist.
   d. The puppy can easily be trained to potty in the house.

24. How is being prepared before you get your puppy helpful? Use evidence from both puppy passages to support your answer.

Houston, Texas

1   Houston, Texas, is a city with many exciting things to do and places to visit. Its museums and monuments provide a great historical background of the area. There are several amusement parks with plenty of games and rides to provide a day of fun for people of all ages. In addition, the city is home to many beautiful parks that host events year-round.

2   Houston's museums are worth checking out. The Natural Museum of Science showcases a variety of dinosaur skeletons, gemstones, and hand-carved artifacts. The Health Museum houses life-size animated organs to teach visitors about healthy lifestyles. Participants can also test their strength and play learning games at the museum. The Children's Museum is an interactive museum for children.

3   If museums aren't exciting enough, visit one of Houston's nearby amusement parks. Spend the day at the Kemah Boardwalk riding a variety of rollercoasters, or ride the Bullet, a high-speed boat that makes a big splash. Pleasure Pier is located 45 miles away on Galveston Island. Carnival rides, games, and restaurants extend out over the water for a thrilling time. Typhoon Texas is an amusement park that offers only water rides. Splash in the wave pool, whoosh down slides, or relax by the pool.

4   If cost is a concern, there are plenty of free parks to visit during a trip to Houston. Memorial Park is known for its miles of hiking and biking trails. Discovery Green is a park that offers seasonal citywide events. During the warmer months, take a stroll through the park, play yard games like cornhole or ring toss, or enjoy a session of outdoor yoga. In the winter, a temporary ice-skating rink is built for all to enjoy. Herman Park is located in the Houston Medical Center. Take a paddleboat in the pond or hang around at the playground. Ride a miniature train around the park and enjoy the beautiful views.

25. Which place in the passage would you like to visit? Use evidence from the passage to support your answer.

26. True or False. The museums discussed are located in Houston. _____

27. Which location offers ice-skating? _____

28. Which of the following would be important to find out before visiting any of the attractions mentioned in the passage?
    a. What size is the dinosaur skeleton?
    b. How much do the tickets cost for children and for adults?
    c. Is chlorine used in the wave pool at the water park?
    d. Is the rollercoaster at the Kemah Boardwalk scary?

29. Which detail is correct?
    a. The Health Museum showcases hand-carved artifacts.
    b. The Kemah Boardwalk is located 45 miles away from Houston on Galveston Island.
    c. Discovery Green offers yoga classes in the winter months.
    d. Children can find gemstones in the Natural Science Museum.

30. The author wrote this passage for which of the following reasons?
    a. To inform travelers about things to do in Houston
    b. To entertain readers while they travel
    c. To advertise for museums and parks in Houston
    d. To convince travelers to avoid visiting Houston

The Rip Runner

1   "I can't do it!" exclaimed John. "I just can't do it!"

2   "Yes, you can! If it wasn't safe, they wouldn't have built it. Look at all the people in line to ride it. They aren't scared." Nathan couldn't believe it. They had finally convinced their parents to let them spend the day here, and now John was getting cold feet.

3   "It's too high. What if I throw up?" John already felt like throwing up. He and Nathan had talked about this moment for months. But he had never dreamed the rollercoaster would be so much taller in person. It sure didn't look that tall on the TV commercial.

4   "You're riding with me, or I'm going to tell Bobby and Mac that you're a big chicken!" cried Nathan. "Let's go!"

5   John didn't want to ruin Nathan's chance to ride the Rip Runner, so he got in line. There were eight people in front of them. If he could just sit down in the car and buckle himself in, maybe he would feel better. Throwing up in front of all of these people would be super embarrassing.

6   They only had to wait 2 minutes before they were climbing into the tram car. John buckled the seat belt and pulled down the shoulder harness. His stomach was in knots. His palms felt sweaty. He should have left a note in his room telling his parents he wanted Nathan to have his Jordans and his bicycle if he died on this rollercoaster.

7   "Are you ready? This is going to be amazing! Here we go!" John yelled as the rollercoaster rounded a tiny bend and paused before it started the slow climb up the hill.

8   John squeezed his eyes shut and held his breath. He didn't need to look over the edge. It would just remind him how high up they were. It seemed like it took 30 minutes to finish the climb, but he could tell by the clicking sound of the rollercoaster that they had made it to the top.

9   "YEE HAW!" John heard Nathan scream.

10   The rollercoaster dropped! Its speed barreled them through twists and turns. The wind whipped through their hair as the coaster turned upside down, doing not one, but two 360-degree loops. It continued its way along the track at top speed until it finally screeched to a stop at the unloading dock.

11   "YEE HAW!" John screamed. "That was awesome! Let's do it again!"

31. How long did John and Nathan have to wait before getting on the ride?
    a. One minute
    b. Two minutes
    c. Three minutes
    d. Four minutes

32. Which of the following sentences is dialogue in the story?
    a. Nathan couldn't believe it.
    b. The rollercoaster dropped!
    c. "Let's go!"
    d. His palms felt sweaty.

33. Why is it important to try new things even if you are scared? Use evidence from the passage to support your answer.

34. Which word is the opposite of *embarrassing*?
    a. Humiliating
    b. Uncomfortable
    c. Upsetting
    d. Enjoyable

35. All except which of the following statements express a reaction John had to being scared?
    a. His stomach was in knots.
    b. His palms felt sweaty.
    c. John buckled the seat belt and pulled down the shoulder harness.
    d. John squeezed his eyes shut and held his breath.

36. Which paragraph contains the most details about the rollercoaster ride?
   a. Paragraph 5
   b. Paragraph 7
   c. Paragraph 8
   d. Paragraph 10

Home

1   "Welcome aboard," said the pilot as the plane took off into the air.

2   It has been the hardest eighteen months of my life. I can't say I didn't know what I was getting myself into, because I did. I knew it would change me. I just didn't know how much it would change me.

3   I used to be different. I was the jerky little kid on your block who did mean things to you all the time. I would let the air out of your bicycle tires when you weren't looking or wrap your house in toilet paper while you were asleep. In high school, I was the kid who failed almost every class and spent most of my lunch periods in detention. I even put a snake in Mrs. Garrett's desk one time.

4   When Dad suggested that I take this job, I wasn't very happy with him. Or maybe I just wasn't happy with myself. I knew I could do better, be nicer, and make people proud of me. I just couldn't figure out how to do it.

5   Being away from home is definitely the hardest part of this job. I'm married now and have two little girls. Kelly is six years old, and Megan is about to turn three. I miss my wife. I miss her home cooking and the strawberry smell of her hair. I can't wait to hug them all and sleep in my own bed.

6   Home is one thing people really forget to appreciate. Where I work, home for most people is a little one-room hut made out of rusty scrap metal. There is no running water or stove for cooking dinners. And there aren't any comfy beds. Everyone sleeps on the dirt floor.

7   The people where I work don't have much of anything. But they have me. I protect them. I keep bad guys from breaking into their huts at night. I keep bad guys from kidnapping them off the streets. I keep bad guys from hurting them. Where I live, people don't have to worry about these dangers.

8   I protect them. That makes me proud to do the job I do. It might be the hardest job I've ever done, but I make a difference in those people's lives. Leaving my family in two months to go back to work will be hard, but it won't be as hard as those people's lives if I don't show back up.

9   "Welcome home to America, soldiers," the pilot said as my plane landed. "Enjoy your time with your families and thank you for your service."

37. Who is telling the story in this passage?
   a. A kid in the neighborhood
   b. A US Army soldier
   c. An airplane pilot
   d. Someone in detention

38. What is the setting of this story?
   a. Home
   b. High school
   c. Neighborhood
   d. Airplane

39. What is the main idea of the passage?
   a. Sometimes jobs are hard, but it makes us feel good to do them.
   b. You should behave when you are a kid, or no one will like you.
   c. Dads are bossy and make you get a job you don't like very much.
   d. If people don't have a good home, invite them to come home with you.

40. What is something you sometimes forget to appreciate about your home? Use evidence from the passage to support your answer.

41. What does the word <u>kidnapping</u> mean?
   a. Releasing
   b. Holding
   c. Snatching
   d. Robbing

42. How long has the solider been away at work? _____

Up, Up, and Away

1   I checked in at the ticket counter and made my way to the airport security line. It was 12:45 p.m., and my flight to Chicago was on time to take off at 2:46 p.m. This wasn't my first time to fly to Aunt Becky's house, but it was my first time to fly alone.

2   I made my way to the airport security line. A lady in front of me was talking on her phone. She was yelling at someone to put the dishes in the dishwasher or they'd be grounded for the rest of their life. The man behind me kept looking at his watch and tapping his foot. I wondered if he was going to be late to catch his flight, but I didn't ask.

3   As I reached the security kiosk, I showed the lady my ticket and my ID card. She waved me through without a smile. As I put my backpack on the x-ray belt, I wondered if she actually liked her job. It sure didn't look like it. I made my way through the metal detector and scooped up my backpack.

4   As I weaved my way around an elderly couple and a lady trying to haul a set of twins through the airport, I read all of the overhead signs. I was looking for gate 16. I only had four more gates to go when one of the airport announcements caught my attention.

5   "Attention, passengers. This is the last call for boarding for flight 972 to Chicago."

6   Oh my! What did she mean last call for boarding? My flight wasn't supposed to leave for another hour and 45 minutes!

7   Panic washed over me as I began to run. Aunt Becky would be worried if I didn't get off the plane in Chicago. When would the next plane leave? What if I had to spend the night in this airport by myself? Thoughts raced through my mind as I ran past the last three gates and came to a stop at the boarding desk at gate 16. I huffed and puffed as I presented my boarding pass to the agent.

8   "You're just in time," she smiled. "We were about to have to push off without you."

9   "Without me?" I gasped. "My ticket says the plane is supposed to leave at 2:46 p.m."

10   "Yes, that is correct. And the time now is 2:35 p.m.," she politely stated.

11   I looked down at my watch. The second hand was no longer moving. I shook my wrist and tapped on the glass. The battery must have died. It must have died at 1:01 p.m.

43. From what point of view is this passage told?

    a. First person
    b. Second person
    c. Third person limited
    d. Third person omniscient

44. Who do you think the lady in the airport security line was talking to on the phone?
    a. Her husband
    b. Her boss
    c. Her child
    d. Her grandma

45. What time was the plane supposed to leave? _____

46. What can you infer about the man in the airport security line?
   a. He was angry.
   b. He was impatient.
   c. He was scared.
   d. He was upset.

47. The solider in the previous passage and the person in this passage had which thing in common?
   a. They were both traveling in an airplane.
   b. They had a train to catch and almost missed it.
   c. They both ate in the airport restaurants.
   d. Aunt Becky would be worried about them if they were late.

48. Write your own sentence using the word <u>weaved</u>.

_____

Hamburger Casserole

Prep time: 5 minutes

Cook time: 30 minutes

Serves: 4

Calories: 365 (1 cup)

1 pound ground beef

1 can cream of mushroom soup

1 can cream of chicken soup

1 can whole kernel corn (drained)

2 teaspoons salt

2 teaspoons ground black pepper

16-ounce bag of egg noodles

12 ounces sour cream

3 tablespoons parsley flakes

1   Boil egg noodles as <u>instructed</u> on the package. Drain noodles when fully cooked. Set aside in a bowl.

2   Use a large skillet to brown ground beef over medium heat until done. Drain excess grease and set aside in a bowl.

3   Mix the following in the skillet: cream of mushroom soup, cream of chicken soup, corn, salt, and pepper. Stir ingredients together, and bring to a light boil, stirring regularly.

4   Reduce heat to simmer. Add egg noodles, ground beef, sour cream, and parsley. Mix well. Simmer for 15 minutes.

5   Suggested sides: salad, green beans, warm rolls.

49. According to this recipe, what is the second step?
    a. Drain noodles.
    b. Mix ingredients.
    c. Reduce to a simmer.
    d. Brown ground beef.

50. Why would the chef need to drain the ground beef? _____

_____

51. How many people will this recipe feed? _____

52. Where might you find this recipe?
   a. A travel magazine
   b. Cookbook
   c. Classified ads
   d. Encyclopedia

53. Which two ingredients would you find close to each other in the grocery store?
   a. Parsley and cream of chicken soup
   b. Ground beef and sour cream
   c. Cream of mushroom soup and cream of chicken soup
   d. Egg noodles and ground black pepper

54. What is a synonym for the word instructed?
   a. Requested
   b. Directed
   c. Suggested
   d. Hinted

Silly Chores

1   Tom,

2   I decided to just write you this letter because I have to leave for work. I just wanted to let you know I did a couple of chores before you woke up. I didn't want you to have to spend all day doing silly jobs to make our house look nice.

4   I emptied the dishwasher. If you are looking for the thermos you use for band camp, it is laying in the driveway next to Dad's boat. Since you are too lazy to put it in the sink when you are done using it, I tossed it back out there. This way, you will know where to find it. I hope bugs don't get in it before you use it.

5   I also did a quick load of laundry. Instead of putting your underwear away, I just threw them back on the floor in your room. You seem to think it's a better place to put them instead of in the dresser drawers, so I left them there. But I think I mixed them with the dirty underwear on the floor since you didn't put your dirty clothes in the hamper. You can always smell them if you need to know which ones are clean.

6   And, you'll never guess what else I did! I picked up all of the things you left in the living room. I figured, since you left them there, you didn't want them. I put them in a trash bag and will drop them off at the donation center on my way to work. Now, you won't have to worry about where to put them anymore.

7   Don't worry! You can thank me later for helping you. If you still haven't figured out how to make your bed by this afternoon, we can just take it out of your room. I'll pick up a sleeping bag on my way home from work just in case.

8   Have a great day, sweetheart!

9   Love,

     Mom

55. Based on the letter Tom's mom wrote, readers can conclude which of the following?
    a. Tom's mom has a job as a clean-up lady.
    b. Tom's mom likes to do all of her housework before work.
    c. Tom's mom is angry because he hasn't been picking up after himself around the house.
    d. Tom's mom is very helpful and loves him.

56. How do you help your parents around the house? Use evidence from the passage to support your answer.

> (blank lined answer area)

57. What is the part of the letter that says "Love, Mom" called?
   a. Body
   b. Closing
   c. Salutation
   d. Heading

58. Instead of smelling all of his underwear, what is another way Tom could handle the situation?
   a. He could sort it all by size and color.
   b. He could put all of his laundry in the dirty clothes hamper.
   c. He could throw all of his underwear away.
   d. He could wash them all together to be sure they are all clean.

59. This letter is written from whose point of view? _____

60. Which task did Tom's mom not take care of before she went to work?
   a. Putting laundry in his room
   b. Putting the thermos outside
   c. Making his bed
   d. Picking up the living room

Answer Explanations #2

1. B: Choice *B* is the only list in alphabetical order.

2. ANSWER: *Walter is doing research on different vacations because he can't decide where to ask his mother to take him.*

3. ANSWER: *Traveling by car is the least expensive.*

4. B: The place where you are going is called a *destination*.

5. SUGGESTED: *Walter's mother will probably choose to take him to Great Wolf Lodge. It is the destination that is the closest and can be easily reached by car. It is not very far from their house. It is also the least expensive at just $876.* (Answers may vary according to student opinion.)

6. C: A newspaper is not a good source of information to use as a research tool for vacations.

7. B: According to Walter's chart in part 1, Great Wolf Lodge is the only water park vacation he researched.

8. A: It is reasonable to think that if Walter wants to go to a water park on vacation, he knows how to swim.

9. ANSWER: *Walter and his mother wore their pajamas at the water park because they went to story time at the end of the day. When you think of story time, you think of getting ready for bed.*

10. A: Paragraph 2 tells readers that buckets of water randomly dumped on Walter's and his mom's heads as they floated around the lazy river.

11. ANSWER: *Paragraph 3 uses the following descriptive words (pick 3): twisted, turned, sloshed, splish-splashed, whooshed.*

12. C: The word <u>bobbled</u> is underlined in paragraph 4. It means "to go up and down."

13. C: This answer covers all of the ideas in the passage. Choices *A, B,* and *D* just refer to specific ideas within the passage.

14. SUGGESTED: *Puppies like to chew on things when they are teething. If they do not have toys to chew on, they might chew on the legs of the furniture.*

15. D: To inspect means "to look at something carefully." If you ignore something, you don't pay any attention to it at all.

16. C: It is likely that a dog trainer would write this passage because trainers are very knowledgeable about dogs. They want to help people understand what it means to correctly take care of a dog.

17. ANSWER: *Paragraph 3 states that you will need puppy shampoo, a brush for dog hair, and a flea collar.*

18. B: This statement is an opinion because it is what someone thinks about puppies. It is not true all the time because many people do not like dogs.

19. B: When you adopt your puppy, an adoption specialist will be able to tell you what kind of food your puppy needs to eat.

20. ANSWER: *If you want to make sure you are getting a full-bred puppy, it is best to look in the classified ads for someone who raises specific breeds.*

21. C: Transitions are words used to move from the idea in one paragraph to a new idea in the next paragraph. Transitions help the text to read smoothly.

22. ANSWER: *It does not cost very much money to adopt a puppy from an animal shelter.*

23. A: If a puppy has been <u>house trained</u>, it has been trained to go to the bathroom outside instead of in the house.

24. SUGGESTED: *It is helpful to be prepared before you get your puppy because it can be overwhelming to pick out a puppy and gather up everything you need all in one day. Your puppy will feel more comfortable in your home if there are toys and a warm bed welcoming him.*

25. SUGGESTED: *I would like to visit Typhoon Texas because I have never been to a water park. I think I would like to ride the tall waterslides. I am a good swimmer, so I know the wave pool would be fun.*

26. True: Each of the museums mentioned are located in Houston, Texas.

27. Discovery Green: Paragraph 4 tells readers that Discovery Green is the place that offers ice-skating in the winter.

28. B: It is important to know how much the tickets cost so you can make sure you have enough money to pay for them when you get there.

29. D: Children can find gemstones in the Natural Science Museum. This detail is found in paragraph 2.

30. A: This is an informational passage. It provides travelers with information about Houston so they can decide if they would like to visit.

31. B: According to paragraph six, the boys had to wait two minutes before getting on the ride.

32. C: When one or more person speaks, it is called dialogue. The author uses quotation marks to show what the character is saying.

33. SUGGESTED: *It is important to try something new even if you are scared because you might end up liking it. John was scared to ride the rollercoaster, but after he did it, he loved it. He even rode it more than once.*

34. D: An antonym is a word that means the opposite. The opposite of *embarrassing* is *enjoyable*.

35. C: John buckled his seat belt because it is a requirement for riding the rollercoaster. He would have to do this even if he wasn't scared.

36. D: Paragraph 10 explains the rollercoaster ride.

37. B: The story is told by an American soldier who is flying home to see his family.

38. D: The story takes place on an airplane.

39. A: The soldier explains how it is hard to be away from his family for so long, but it makes him proud to know that he protects people.

40. SUGGESTED: *Sometimes I forget to appreciate that we have a lot of furniture at our house. I have a bed big enough for three people, and it has a lot of pillows on it. I think it would be terrible to have to sleep on the hard floor, especially if it was just dirt.*

41. C: The word kidnapping means "to snatch someone up and take them away so no one can find them."

42. Eighteen months: In paragraph 2, the soldier says the past eighteen months have been very hard. Readers can conclude that the soldier has been away for that long.

43. A: First-person point of view means someone is telling a story about themselves. The word *I* is used in first-person stories.

44. C: A child is the only person the lady would threaten to ground for not putting the dishes in the dishwasher.

45. 2:46 p.m.: Paragraph 1 and paragraph 9 both state that the plane was supposed to take off at 2:46 p.m.

46. B: Looking at your watch and tapping your foot usually mean you don't have time or don't want to spend the time doing something. These details help the reader infer that the man was impatient.

47. A: The soldier in the previous story and the person in the current story are both traveling on an airplane.

48. SUGGESTED: *The lady weaved the needle back and forth through the fabric as she sewed up the hole.*

49. A: Draining the noodles is the second step in the cooking process.

50. ANSWER: When ground beef is cooked, there is usually excess fat in the pan. This should be drained because it won't taste very good in the casserole.

51. 4: This recipe will feed four people according to the notes at the top of the recipe.

52. B: Most recipes can be found in cookbooks.

53. C: More than likely, the cream soups will be located near each other on the same aisle in the grocery store.

54. B: *Directed* is a word that means the same as *instructed*.

55. C: Tom probably hasn't been doing his chores, so his mom got angry and took some extreme measures to make a point.

56. SUGGESTED: *I help my mom clean the bathrooms, and I have to take out the trash. My mom also likes for me to make my bed just like Tom's mom likes him to make his bed.*

57. B: The closing of a letter includes the signature.

58. D: Tom could wash all of his underwear, and then he would know they are all clean.

59. Mom: This letter is written from Mom's point of view. She talks about observations she has noticed about Tom's chores.

60. C: Tom's mother suggests that he make his bed before she gets home, or he will have to use a sleeping bag.

Dear Customer,

Thank you for purchasing this book. We hope that we exceeded your expectations.

Our goal in creating this book was to cover all of the topics that are likely to appear on the test. We also strove to make our practice questions as similar as possible to what will be seen on test day. With that being said, if you found something that you feel was not up to your standards, please send us an email and let us know.

We have study guides in a wide variety of fields. If you're interested in one, try searching for it on Amazon or send us an email.

FSA Grade 3 Math Workbook	amazon.com/dp/1628456507
Grade 3 Math Workbook	amazon.com/dp/1628454660

Thanks Again and Happy Testing!
Product Development Team
info@studyguideteam.com

Interested in buying more than 10 copies of our product? Contact us about bulk discounts:

bulkorders@studyguideteam.com

FREE Test Taking Tips DVD Offer

To help us better serve you, we have developed a Test Taking Tips DVD that we would like to give you for FREE. **This DVD covers world-class test taking tips that you can use to be even more successful when you are taking your test.**

All that we ask is that you email us your feedback about your study guide. Please let us know what you thought about it – whether that is good, bad or indifferent.

To get your **FREE Test Taking Tips DVD**, email freedvd@studyguideteam.com with "FREE DVD" in the subject line and the following information in the body of the email:

    a. The title of your study guide.

    b. Your product rating on a scale of 1-5, with 5 being the highest rating.

    c. Your feedback about the study guide. What did you think of it?

    d. Your full name and shipping address to send your free DVD.

If you have any questions or concerns, please don't hesitate to contact us at freedvd@studyguideteam.com.

Thanks again!

Made in the USA
Monee, IL
07 March 2020

22855132R00063